Shatte

The True Story of a Child Soldier

Thank you for your support
love Essi
778-891-2273

Essi Bagheri

Copyright © 2018

All Rights Reserved

ISBN: 9781074711375

Dedication

There are so many people I can dedicate this book to, from children who lost their lives in a battlefield to people who suffered from physical, sexual, and emotional abuse, I dedicate this book to men and woman who are still suffering from violence and innocent children who were killed in the suicide mission I witnessed in Iran in my life.

Acknowledgment

There are so many people I want to thank, and I will start with Savey Mattu and his wife, Nicole Taylor. Without Savey, I wouldn't be here. He has been my friend and brother, and I can't put into words the tremendous gratitude that I feel for Savey. I want to thank him for believing in me and supporting me for many years and in many ways.

I also want to express my heartfelt thanks to another friend and brother, Juggy. It is difficult to know where to start describing how he loved me and cared for me in so many ways. Without his support, kindness, and generosity, I would not be here to thank him altogether.

I acknowledge my friend and brother Tony, along with his wife Yvonne Roberts, who loved me and watched over me, while I was in and out of treatment, mentoring me without ever judging me.

Kim Bartley, who supported me and believed in me, always encouraging me not to give up.

I will always be grateful to my friend Jillian West for her support throughout this project.

There are so many others who I should also thank, but I

will conclude by expressing my gratitude to Jacquie Jordan (TV Guestpert, Los Angeles), Marty Steckdaub, Julie Weiss Torrieri, and Guy T. Britten. Additionally, I want to name Neils Haley, Alex Cupi, Nadine, Anthony, Colleen Clandening, Jordan Boehm, Lisa Stitchman , photo credit goes to Richard Glen Lett, with special thanks to my friend Elizabeth Ridley for her time and support..

About the Author

Child sexual assault victim. Boy soldier. Teen father. Adult recovering drug addict.

Essi Bagheri has lived a thousand lifetimes in his relatively short years. Born in Iran, in 1966, Essi was a young, vibrant boy whose world was shattered when he was brutally assaulted by a family friend. Seeking to escape and redeem himself, he was brainwashed into joining the Revolutionary Guard. But he became disillusioned when he watched his close childhood friends be blown to smithereens by landmines.

Desperate to escape, he shot himself in the arm – only to be honorably discharged and treated as a hero. What followed was a lifetime of hiding, running, drug addiction and alcoholism across four continents as Essi attempted to outrun his past and his shame. But it's only when his path of self-destruction found him living on the streets amongst the most downtrodden, that Essi finally found forgiveness and redemption.

Today, Essi is sober and clean. He lives a full and happy life in Vancouver, BC, Canada. He is a motivational speaker and spends his time and energy helping others recover from their traumas and addictions. For more information about Essi visit www.donotgiveupnow.com

Preface

I thank you from the bottom of my heart in advance for taking your time and reading my book. It's been a challenging and therapeutic journey to talk about my life. I hope that by reading this book, you will have more gratitude for life and where you in it at this moment; and why I wrote this book is to inspire and inform my readers that we are in this life for a short amount of time and no matter how tough and challenging life gets, we can always overcome it.

This is the story of a child and circumstances of culture, religion, and human disconnection; and how we can love one another and live in peace in spite of the challenging circumstances; in spite of what other people think about us by crushing the old belief system and creating a new one as we go along. This is the story of a child who faced separation physically and emotionally, and was sexually abused and brainwashed to do unthinkable deeds. It is also the journey of a refugee's escape from mental health issues, addiction and final recovery. I hope this book would inspire you to love and to cherish one another.

Contents

Dedication i
Acknowledgment ii
About the Author iv
Preface vi
Chapter 1- On Being a Child – The Beginning 1
Chapter 2- The Uprising – Iran in Turmoil 23
Chapter 3- My Life after the War 44
Chapter 4- An Unexpected Journey 58
Chapter 5- My Journey to Turkey and Beyond 73
Chapter 6- Moving to Canada and Continuing My Personal Battle ... 90
Chapter 7- A New Destination – Vancouver 110
Chapter 8- The Road to Healing 131

Chapter 1
On Being a Child – The Beginning

*"The heart dies a slow death, shedding each hope like leaves until one day there are none. No hopes. Nothing remains." – **Arthur Golden***

This saying by Arthur Golden describes my life the best. It cannot get more poetic than this. It's challenging to find a quote, a saying that can sum up a life like mine. My life is punctuated with so much pain, guilt, shame, and despair that sometimes even I get startled by the fact that I am still alive. How did I even survive? How much pain and suffering can a man endure? How much of turmoil and chaos can a man live through in his life? If there's a limit to it, I think I have hit that limit.

A life like mine is not ordinary. And it's certainly not worth living. What else is a person supposed to say when he doesn't have a purpose of living? I felt I was the loneliest person in the world. For years, I had to live with that feeling. But even now that I have found purpose in my life, it still is difficult for me to put my story into words. I don't think if I can bear the rush of feelings that comes with talking about my life. Reflecting on my life experiences and reminiscing about what I have been through is a difficult task to undertake, but I must try. I must try for the good of people like me out there. Yes, I help people whose lives are as miserable as my life was. I help people who fall in life, get up, and then fall again. Just like I did. I had no one to help me out, and that's why I know how badly people like me need the right kind of help at the right time. I made my weakness my strength. I made my disease my power. It took time, and it wasn't easy, but I learned how to stand up on my feet again. And that's why I feel like sharing my story with the world. I muster all my strength to tell the people who have been through the worst of the worst in their lives that you must never give up. Learn from my experiences and never give up. No matter what challenges your life throws at you.

After traveling around the world, hopeless and shattered, I came to Canada in 1988. Now, I live in Vancouver, a Canadian city to die for. The beauty of this place is incomparable. Sometimes when I wake up in the morning and experience the city, it reminds me of Esfahan, the Iranian town I grew up in. The mountains, the snowy winters, the air, the clouds, and the lakes and valleys of this place bring back my childhood memories of Esfahan. I'm an Iranian, and I had to go through a lot to get to Vancouver. It has been quite a journey, both literally and emotionally. And this book is about my journey. But I don't want to start off talking about myself. First, I want you to understand my dysfunctional family. I want you to know what my parents were like before I start talking about what I went through when I was just a child.

So allow me to share a short story about my father and how he married my mother back in Iran. That should set the tone of my story.

My father, Ramzan, was a worker in a cement company in Shiraz. The year was 1962. One day, one of his co-workers who was also his friend saw a girl with her family, and he told my father that he liked that girl. She was a young girl. The friend somehow managed to get her family's address and gave it to my father. He wanted my father to meet the family and talk to them about him. He wanted my father to arrange his marriage with that girl. But when my father went to meet the family, he was so smitten by my mother's beauty that he ended up asking for her hand. He said he was interested in marrying her. In short, my father didn't give his friend's proposal and arranged his marriage. My mother told me this story not a long time ago.

My mother, Zahra, was not even 12 years old. She was 11 years and 7 months old to be precise when my father, who was 30 to 32 years old at the time, married her. But that marriage would not bring my mother happiness. She didn't even know what was happening to her.

How my father married my mother is not the only shocking thing. My mother and her family were not aware of the fact that my father was already married. He had a wife, Nosrat, and two children, a daughter also named Zahra and a son named Abrahim, who lived in Esfahan.

It won't be wrong to say that my father used his charm to fool my mother's family. My maternal grandparents were impressed by my father's mature and well-spoken demeanor. By the time my mother's family found out that my father was already married, it was too late. My mother had already become my father's second wife. Having more than one wife was acceptable in Iran at that time in both legal and religious terms. After a while, my father took his new bride back to his home in Esfahan and introduced her to Nosrat and his two children. Soon, both wives found themselves living with one another under the same roof. Of course, Nosrat wasn't happy that this young and beautiful woman was now the second wife of her husband and was living with them. I can understand her feelings. No woman wants to share her husband. But she had to. She had no choice.

I don't know the exact details of how my mother got along with Nosrat and how she treated my mother in the house. Still, sensing the gravity of the situation, I can assume that my mother had to go through a tough time, trying to adjust in the family. The thing that unsettles me the most is that she was so young when she had to go through this phase.

Time passed, and life continued, and my mother gave birth to my older sister, Mehry, who died for some reason soon after her birth. That was a disturbing event for my mother. You can imagine how severe the loss of a first-born child is for a mother. It's irreplaceable. After some time, I was born, a son. My mother must have been so happy. She must have expected so much of me. But it wasn't until I was born when the real tragedy struck both my mother and me. That tragedy was the first blow to me. My first trauma. Come to think of it, it's bizarre to say that because I was a newborn, and I didn't even know what was happening, but this unfair tragedy impacted me. It affected me in ways you cannot imagine.

My mother told me that when I was only six months old, and Zahra was a year and a half, she took us both to Shiraz to visit her family. Now, I don't have memories of this incident because I was still wrapped in my mother's arms, but from what I have heard, we were having a good time with my mother's family. But the trip was ruined for us all when my father gave my mother a surprise.

It wasn't his sudden visit that took my mother by surprise. It was the news that he brought with him that startled her and her family. It was as if a lightning bolt had struck the family. My mother, she tells me, was stunned into silence. She was utterly bowled over when my father blatantly accused her of infidelity, something that is taken very seriously in a conservative Islamic country like Iran. My father in a fit of rage and fury accused my mother of having an illicit relationship with some other man. My grandparents tried to calm him down and settle the issue, but he was consumed with nothing but hatred for her. He was in no mood for understanding the counter-arguments put forward by my mother in her defense. She tried to convince him that he must have had a misunderstanding but to no avail. Back in those days, women had no rights.

In Iran, they certainly didn't. It was a patriarchal society, and whatever a man had to say was given preference. Thus, my mother was left in tears. Her arguments were not enough for my father. She could not satisfy my father with whatever she had to say to prove her innocence, and in just a moment, her life was ruined. As a result of this allegation, my mother was dragged to the court of law. And since there wasn't enough evidence to prove her innocence, she went to jail. And I got separated from my mother.

When I think of this incident now, I thank god that it all happened before the Islamic Revolution. Had it happened after the *Enqelabe Iran,* my mother would have been stoned to death. At least, my mother saved, for which I'm thankful. But the separation was unpardonable. Now that I am in a better position to understand the cruelty of this act, I can understand what horrible impact it must have had on me. *I was only six months old, and my mother was taken away from me. That's something not supposed to happen to a six-month-old child. I didn't know what was happening. I didn't even know my mother then, to take notice of her absence. But I guess there's something like feeling as well. I must have sensed her absence. I must have longed for her touch. I must have missed the comfort my mother used to give me. It's just that I couldn't say it out loud. I couldn't express all that. There's no denying the fact that too much was taken away from me. I'm sure the separation from my mother is somewhat responsible for how I grew up.*

All I know is that I didn't deserve that. It's not just fair. I think no six-month-old baby deserves to be separated from the mother. But you know the ugly truth – the world doesn't stop spinning if a newborn baby is snatched from the comforts of a mother's embrace. Life continues. And so did mine. Following the tragedy that had befallen me, my father took Zahra and me back to Esfahan, and Nosrat raised me. When I took hold of my senses, I knew that Nosrat was my birth mother, and Abrahim and Zahra were my brother and sister. And with that understanding, my childhood began.

I don't know who gave my father the license to toy with my emotions at such an impressionable age of mine. I was about five or six years old when I found out about my birth mother. I have a faint memory of me playing outside in beautiful, sunny weather when my father came to me and brought me inside. Nosrat was there too. He sat me down and told me the most hard-hitting truth of my life. There was something in his voice that warned me that something terrible was coming my way.

As it turned out, it wasn't bad. It was nerve-shattering. I don't know why exactly my father told me that, but he did. Maybe he wanted to tell me about my mother because she had served her jail sentence and was released, or perhaps it was just another attempt to knock my senses out. Whatever the reason was, it was like my heart skipped a beat, as those words fell out of my father's mouth. It was like the world stood still for a while.

It was another emotional jerk that I got. It was a lot to take in. The woman I thought was my mother was not my mother. The boy and girl I thought were brother and sister were not my siblings. But that wasn't the worst part. The worst and the most disturbing lie someone ever told me was about to follow. I was made to believe that my birth mother left me when I was very young. I was devastated to say the very least. I remember my knees going weak. Words failed me, and I stood speechless. You can very well imagine how I must have felt. It was as if my whole existence was nullified. I keep that chapter in my life bookmarked because that's when my life became a spiral to hell. When I sat alone and thought about this life-changing revelation, I couldn't think of a plausible reason as to why my mother would have abandoned me. Did she not like me? Did she not want me? What did I ever do to upset her so much that she left me? I was young, and my young mind could not think of a better reason. So I ended up getting angry at myself and blaming myself for whatever happened. It must have been me because of who my mother left. The idea of mothers leaving their infantile children was new to me. I had never heard of such an instance before. The lie that was fed to my mind got me believing that somehow it was my fault. I must have been not good enough for her.

As shaken as my world had become, I was barely interested in doing anything else. I didn't want to play, I didn't want to eat, I didn't want to study, and I could hardly sleep. The only thing I knew was that my whole life was a colossal lie. I didn't know who I was anymore. All of a sudden, there was a big question mark over my identity.

The next episode of this phase in my life saw me visiting my birth mother. My father took me to Shiraz to meet my birth mother, Zahra, and her family. I'd be lying if I say that I was excited to see my mother. The whole experience was extremely confusing for me. I had no memory of my mother. I had no idea what she looked like. There were so many questions in my mind. I didn't know what I would say when she meets me. I didn't know how I'll respond when she lovingly hugs me or runs her hand over my head. When we reached my mother's house, I was feeling tense. My hands and feet were cold, and I had tears in my eyes. I was nervous, I was scared, and I was emotional. What a rush of emotions it was. When I was unexpectedly introduced to a mother and grandparents I never knew I had I could barely lift my eyes. It would probably be difficult for most adults as well to come to terms with such shocking news about their family relationships.

In my case, as a little boy, these developments raised issues of acceptance and abandonment that would remain with me for the rest of my life. When my mother took my name, I couldn't hold my tears back. She came closer to me and sat down on the floor so she could look at my face. She cupped my face and lifted my face. The first thing I noticed was that she had tears in her eyes as well. It was relieving to know that I wasn't the only one who was on the verge of an emotional breakdown. She was quiet, but the tears in her eyes spoke volumes.

I wasn't able to decipher the meaning of those tears, but now when I think of that moment, I know it was her way of telling me that she didn't leave me. She never abandoned me. My mother gently kissed my forehead and hugged me. I hugged her back. Later, we talked about different things. My mother asked me about my interests, what I liked to eat, and what color I liked the most. I was young, but I was able to realize the strong connection with my mother. Even though we had only known each other for a brief six-month period right after I was born, I could feel that I was an integral part of her. She kept talking to me the entire day to break my hesitation, but she never dared to burden me with the truth, the truth behind her absence in my life. She knew I was going through enough already. She knew it would be difficult for me to process the fact. She knew I was dealing with a lot at that moment, so she stayed quiet, instead of disturbing me further that very day. She revealed the truth to me after many years. I guess that's how deep a mother's love is for her child. She must be dying to clear my misunderstandings, but she chose not to and protected my already troubled mind. I stayed there for a day or two, and then my father brought me back with him to Esfahan.

There are days when I think about the day I met my mother. I can't help imagine how my life would've been if my mother was not separated from me. Everything would have been different. My childhood would have been better.

The life in Esfahan was pretty much the same. I used to think of my mother. Her beautiful face never left my mind. All I had to do was close my eyes, and her face would appear in my mind. I think that longing for my mother made me a restless kid. My problem was I didn't know where I belong. The reason why I felt that way was I didn't have an enjoyable parent-child experience. Even though Nosrat was a good woman, used to take good care of me, and treated me as one of her own, she used to work as a housekeeper for affluent families, which kept her outside most of the day. She would bring food from there. My grandma also worked in luxurious houses as well. I felt shame that Nosrat had to work in other people's homes. The very thought that she was sweating while cleaning a wealthy family's house disturbed me a lot. In return, I wanted good things to happen to Nosrat.

My father used to go to Kuwait for months. He worked in Kuwait and sent us money. When Baba used to come home, he brought Zahra, Abrahim, and me some toys, which would take my mind off things and make me happy for the time being. But if truth be told, I was never close to my father. I never forgave him for what he did to my mother. When I came to know about my mother, I never asked my father why he did what he did. Was it to get rid of her? Was she having an affair? Whatever it was, I didn't want to give him a chance to explain himself. He didn't even once think of what will happen to me if my mother would go to jail. How inconsiderate and self-centered it was of him.

Even though my childhood seems like it was ages ago, and I have come a long way from Iran as well, not a day goes by when I don't think about my childhood, and how the early years of my life were. After all, whatever I am today is because of what happened to me back then. A lot of things remind me of the time that I spent in Iran. Sometimes when I drink tea, flashbacks of my childhood in Esfahan rewind in my mind. When I see children playing in the streets, I recall the games that I grew up playing back in Esfahan.

Yes, I had an outdoor life in Esfahan. That was my only way to escape the turmoil in my life. I had a friend named Essi. You can see that both of us had the same name. We used to play soccer and go to the movies together. I remember that even though Essi and I were good friends and playmates, I often felt jealous of him. He seemed to be a part of a loving family, and I was not. He had the most important and valuable thing that I wanted as well, parental love.

I used to steal money from my father's pockets and go to watch movies with Essi. I spent that money on watching movies and treating my friends. Also, one day, when I was looking for something in a closet where blankets and bedding items were stored, I felt something was kept inside a pillowcase. When I took out the pillowcase, I discovered it was full of money. From that day onwards, I started stealing money from there. I don't know why that money was there. Every once in a while I would take money from that pillowcase and go out with my friends. That was perhaps some of the best days of my life. Little did I know those days were numbered and would soon come to an end!

I thought I had a good friend, but not even my friend could save me from walking on the path of self-destruction because a few years later, I was saddened to hear that he had become a drug addict and died. What a travesty. What a loss it was. That was the point where I started to believe that I was cursed. I must be cursed. Nothing or no one enjoyable stays with me. Nothing good happens to me. I felt I was the unluckiest person walking on the face of this world.

I was eight years old when we moved to Dizicheh, a small village in the countryside. My grandmother became sick and told my dad that when she died, she wanted to be back where she was born, in the country on a farm area. I was used to the city, and all my friends were there, so I wasn't happy about leaving and settling down in the country. However, when I went there, I realized that Dizicheh was a pleasant rural village in Esfahan. At that time, my father owned an 18-wheeler semi-trailer truck. Since he had come back from Kuwait and had quite a bit of money, he had status and was highly regarded in the countryside. Everyone used to call him "Mr. Bagheri." Abrahim also used to work with my father.

As for me, I was growing up, but not without troubles. I was good at ping pong, but I wasn't very good at my school subjects. Moreover, I was not getting along with Abrahim. He was older than me, and as far as I can remember, he was always angry about one thing or another. He used to torment me all the time. Sometimes we used to fight over food, sometimes over games, and sometimes for no good reason.

When I got older and learned to defend myself, my arguments with Abrahim turned into fights. Not even our father was spared from Abrahim's anger. He used to fight a lot with him as well. There was a lot of yelling and screaming in the family. With so much tension, I became quite a rebel at school as well. I used to fight with other kids. Sometimes I used to get beaten badly, and sometimes I used to beat my opponents. It was a rough life I was living. Then for a brief while, things got slightly better when Zahra's marriage was arranged.

Zahra got married to a man named Ali Nazari. She went to Abadan, an Iranian city near the Iraq border. When they used to visit us, I enjoyed it a lot. That was because I started having fun with my brother-in-law. He and I bonded well. He was kind to me and made me laugh. Finally, I had someone in my life to get inspired by, someone to look up to. But as usual, I didn't know I was running out of my share of good days. Soon I was about to face the most terrible horror of my life. Never in my wildest dreams had I ever thought something like that would happen to me. When I was nine, my father decided that it would be good if I visited Zahra and Ali for a few days. Perhaps he was sick and tired of my fights with Abrahim. I also felt it would be a nice change, so I accepted the offer. My father trusted one of his distant friends to take me to Abadan one day in his truck. His friend used to deliver goods from one city to another in his vehicle. Since we had quite a long distance ahead of us, we hit the road before noon. I got along fine with the driver as our journey started. We talked to each other about Iran, our families, my schooling, and other different topics. However, the thing I was enjoying the most was the view. I had never been out on such long routes and passing by various cities, and villages truly made my day.

I had only traveled to Shiraz, which isn't very far from Esfahan. That was the first time I was traveling across the country. Since the trip was of about 10 to 12 hours, I was having the time of my life on the road. We passed by beautiful landscapes, including the mountains in Lordegan and the rivers in Dehdez. I thoroughly enjoyed experiencing the beauty of Iran. I realized that it was true what they said about Iran's natural beauty. It was indeed beyond comparison.

I asked the driver endless questions about every village and city that we passed by. Since he used to travel these roads frequently, he seemed to have extensive knowledge about every town and village. We stopped briefly for a quick lunch and kahwa and continued with our journey. We had been traveling for about six to seven hours. The sun had already set when the driver told me he wanted to rest for a while. Considering the guy was driving for so long, I thought it was fair enough. Even I felt a little tired. The driver stopped along the way and pulled off onto a side road to take a nap. He insisted me to take a power nap, saying it would freshen me up for the rest of the journey. I had nothing else to do. So, I didn't see any harm in joining the driver in the back of the truck and taking a nap. I was tired, and I dozed off within a few minutes.

What happened next is very difficult for me to talk about or even think about it. It happened so fast that I barely remember the details. I was fast asleep on the floor of the truck when suddenly I woke up, sensing some weight on me. When I opened my eyes, I was lying face down on the floor with a greasy hand covering my mouth so that I don't scream. I tried to struggle, but the driver was too strong for me. To keep me still on the floor, the driver slipped his arm around my neck and choked me to the point of making me feel dizzy. I couldn't breathe.

I felt suffocated is what I remember. I couldn't resist so I lay motionless. I could smell his sweat. I could feel his hands all over me. The weight of his body kept me pinned to the floor so hard that I could barely move a muscle. He had pulled down my pants, and he was done raping me in the next few minutes. I didn't understand the concept of sexual assault. I just knew that the guy was hurting me, and I was in terrible pain. When he was finished, I didn't even have the energy to get up. My eyes were wet, and I was gasping for air. Then I started to cry. I was trembling. I was alone. I was frightened. The guy got up and pulled his pants up, telling me to keep my mouth shut.

This guy went on and molested me. The guilt and shame that came with it I can never forget. I felt my innocence was ripped off me that night in the truck. That was another devastating moment of my life. It left me horrorstruck. I wanted to go home. I wanted my mother. I wanted to get out of there. When we reached Abadan, I didn't tell anyone what happened to me. The shame and humiliation weighed me down. I didn't know how to put that experience into words. I was too ashamed and felt no one would believe me. Most boys and girls and women who get raped don't talk about it. And I did the same thing. I remained quiet and allowed the incident to haunt me for the rest of my life.

I was just nine years of age when my childhood came to an end. When I arrived at Zahra's house, I didn't say a word to her. I kept that horrible secret to myself for many years. Looking back now, I realize how that single unspeakable incident has damaged me. And how it led to my years of self-

destructive behavior.

It was as if I hadn't gone through enough already. There was more pain and suffering in store for me. Whatever that was left of my childhood was taken away by Ali, Zahra's husband. The guy I thought was good and kind to me began to throw tantrums at me. While I was in Abadan, I had to endure my brother-in-law's severe beating. It turned out that he had become addicted to opium. While high on the drug, he took leave of his senses and did whatever he pleased. During my stay in Abadan, I used to get terrified when it was time for him to come home.

One evening, Ali came home and grabbed me from the back of my neck. He dragged me inside the house and pushed me hard. I fell on the floor. He was severely drunk and not in his senses. He unfastened his belt and whipped me with it brutally. I still don't know the reason why he beat me. It must be for some slights that he thought I had done. Zahra tried to stop him, but he was too fierce and wild. She kept trying to hold his hand back, but he kept shoving her away like a barbarian. She cried and begged Ali to spare me from this horror but to no avail. The same thing happened several times. I was beaten with a belt by Ali like a savage.

Consequently, I became incredibly quiet. I barely spoke

to anyone and chose to stay away from everyone. Zahra later told me that Ali's business was on the verge of collapse, and he was under serious debt. People used to come to him for their money, and Ali had none to give them back. As a result, he had found solace in opium and alcohol. But that didn't justify Ali's barbaric behavior. I was so utterly disappointed in him and disturbed by the way he used to beat me that I felt I would never be able to trust anyone again. Later, when Ali was done with beating me, I used to spend hours and hours crying alone. There was no one to listen to me. There was no one to understand my loneliness. There was no one to listen to my cries. There were times when I felt even God had abandoned me for some reason. There was no place I could go to and feel safe and be happy. There was no corner in this world that was safe for me. I felt wherever I went, my misfortune followed me. I had practically lost all hope in life by now.

People say time heals every wound. I say time doesn't heal every wound. Some injuries leave marks on you for you to remember them as long as you live. I got such bruises at a very young age. They will never heal, and they will remind me of what I went through. Whenever I hear an incident that involves child molestation or child abuse, a shiver runs down my spine. The thing that saddens me the most is that despite all the awareness, such crimes never seem to stop. It hurts me a lot.

Chapter 2
The Uprising – Iran in Turmoil

"If you want to forget something or someone, never hate it, or never hate him/her. Everything and everyone that you hate is engraved upon your heart; if you want to let go of something, if you want to forget, you cannot hate." – ***C. Joybell***

And that's what I couldn't do. I couldn't stop hating what happened to me, and that's why I couldn't forget. I returned home from Abadan with a heavy heart. I knew what Ali did to me would stay with me forever; like a wound that never heals. I could feel it in my bones that I would never be able to forget what happened on this trip I had embarked upon so excitedly. I just cursed myself for giving in to temptation and leaving home. I shouldn't have left home in the first place. None of this would have happened. I wouldn't have traveled in that truck, and I wouldn't have seen the dark side of Ali's temperament.

I never said a word to Nosrat or my father. I stayed quiet. I never talked about the incident in the truck, and I never mentioned the physical abuse I suffered at the hands of Ali.

But I knew I was far from being healed. The torment I went through was insufferable. While lying in bed at night, I used to cry. I used to cry myself to sleep every night. Maybe not telling anyone about anything was a mistake, but I wasn't sure if anyone would understand what I went through. I felt no one would be able to help me, and all I'll get would be some sympathy and pity, which was of no use. I felt ashamed of what happened to me and deep down blamed myself for everything. I blamed myself for not fighting back hard enough to stop the driver from molesting me. I blamed myself for letting it happen to me by not fighting him back. That's what a victim of sexual assault suffers from. And I didn't know that back then. All I knew was that I wouldn't be able to express my feelings in the right way, so I ended up staying quiet. I lived in a small village where everyone knew each other by name. Had I told anyone what happened to me, it would have become the talk of the town. Everyone would gossip. And I didn't want anyone to reassure my guilt and shame by saying something like you should have tried to resist or scream for help.

Now when I think about it, I realize how wrong I was. The guy never gave me a chance to fight back or scream for help. I was innocent. I was helpless. It wasn't my fault; I was just a 9-year-old kid. I wish I could've thought like that back then.

If so, I would've stopped blaming myself, and things would've been different today.

So I had no role model, no one to look up to in the hour of need. Ali was way too consumed by rage and fury to be friends with me again. I was going through the first phase of depression except that I was too young to name it, too young to even identify that I was suffering from depression. Seeing everyone around me walking and talking and living life usually kind of bothered me. Everyone was happy and content with the routine. There were three or four types of dishes prepared for dinner at my house every day. The dinner was followed by a round of Persian tea, as usual. Nosrat would clean the dishes after meals, while my father used to play cards and drink or smoke opium with his friends.

There were times when I felt I should open myself up to Nosrat, but I couldn't. My hesitation and shame always came in between and stopped me. If there was someone who could understand me, it was her. I felt like unburdening the weight on my heart by telling everything to her, but I never did. Just seeing her working around the house all day comforted me.

Nosrat was a devoted Muslim. She was religious and a good mom. She used to wash my clothes with hands every day. She used to fetch water every day because we were living in a village. Sometimes I wondered if she was a godsend. There was no proper kitchen in our house, and she used to cook on fire that she created with woods. Eating the meals she had prepared with her hands was the only good thing in my life. I loved it when she made mixed rice with lamb or beef. Even though I have little memories of that time, I still remember the taste of her food. She used to make the most delicious yogurt that we had at breakfast. I sincerely believe she did what she could to raise me in a disciplined manner. And that's why I still like and respect her. She may not be the mother who gave birth to me, but she's the one who raised me with love and care.

That doesn't mean I don't value my birth mother. The traumas of my life may have washed away most of my memory of that time. However, I still faintly remember my frequent visits to Shiraz to Zahra, my birth mother, and her family. It was a small village in Shiraz where everyone knew each other. During my short visits, the villagers had grown so accustomed to me that they used to call me *"Son of Shiraz."*

My mother's family was a big one. I had a grandmother there, an aunt, and three uncles who were my mother's brothers. My eldest uncle had a snack shop in a local movie theatre where he served sandwiches, ice cream, and popcorn.

Whenever I visited Shiraz, he used to take me to the movie theatre where I watched free Iranian movies. It used to be a pleasant change. I thought watching movies helped you explore the world around you. It involved you in the lives of fictional characters and made you forget your own life for a while. That's why I loved the whole idea of making movies and watching movies. I don't exactly remember how many movies I watched in that theatre. All I remember is that those were some relieving moments in my complicated life. But of course, that was before the revolution. With my mother's family, I had fun. My uncles liked me, and I started feeling loved too. They showed me around the village and talked to me about different things, just random stuff about how life was in Shiraz. I felt important when I was with my uncles because they thought of me as someone who had a mind of his own and had opinions. They told me how the whole political scenario of the country was on the brink of a radical change. They were the first ones who told me about the impending uprising in Iran. Sadly, my visits to Shiraz didn't last long. Those were short visits, and they would end soon. But at least, I thought I had something positive going on in my life that I could look forward to for a change. The emphasis is on *thought* because I didn't know that Iran was inching towards a catastrophe that would change the entire country forever.

You must have guessed what that catastrophe was. A revolution was brewing in Iran, and it erupted with full force in 1979. I was still a 13-year-old kid who had no clear idea as to what was happening in the country. Some people were in favor of the Islamic revolution, while others were against it. I remember that I found the words of a famous singer very moving. He sang about prophets and inspired people to fight and die for their religion and beliefs. The country was in chaos as the winds brought the scent of the blood and cries of people in the air. The revolution caused severe bloodshed. Thousands of civilians lost their lives in the civil war that broke out. I remember watching the news with my family about the riots taking place in the country. People gathered to attack the U.S. embassy in Tehran. I had little understanding of what the revolution was about. I didn't know what it meant to live in the Islamic Republic. I had little idea about who Ayatollah Khomeini was. I didn't know about Islam, despite my mother being a devout Muslim woman who prayed five times a day. The most I did was visit a mosque, but I wasn't a very religious person at the time.

Everyone's eyes were fixed on the television. The country was changing. When I saw everybody's eyes glued to the screen, I couldn't help take mine off as well. Hordes of people came out in the streets of Tehran and other cities, chanting *"Marg bar Shah"* or *"Death to the Shah"*, and *"Death to America!"* Middle-class Iranians, university students, and Islamist supporters of Ayatollah Khomeini united under one banner to overthrow Shah Mohammad Raza Pahlavi, a figure many Iranians called a puppet installed by the USA. The people of Iran wanted to end the monarchy because hunger and poverty were taking over the country. On January 16, 1979, Shah Mohammad Reza Pahlavi announced that he and his wife were going abroad for a brief vacation. Crowds of happy people took to the streets as their plane took off. The people in various cities began tearing down statues and pictures of Shah and his family. Prime Minister Shapour Bakhtiar (who had been in office for just a few weeks) agreed to free all political prisoners, ordered the army to stand down in the face of demonstrations, and abolished the SAVAK, the secret intelligence organization of Iran. Also, the Prime Minister also allowed the then exiled Ayatollah to return to the country and called for free elections.

Khomeini flew into Tehran from Paris on February 1, 1979, to an excited welcome. Once he was safely inside the country's borders, Khomeini called for the dissolution of the Bakhtiar government, vowing *"I shall kick their teeth in."*

He appointed a prime minister and cabinet of his own. From February 9-10, fighting broke out between the Imperial Guard (the "Immortals"), who were still loyal to the Shah, and the pro-Khomeini faction of the Iranian Air Force. On February 11, the pro-Shah forces collapsed, and the Islamic Revolution declared victory over the Pahlavi dynasty. Of course, I learned all of this later when I was an adult.

After the revolution, the government wasn't political; it was purely religious. Now that I think of it, the new Islamic regime was a bit extreme in their views. For instance, veil or *hijaab* was made compulsory for Iranian women of all ages, and there were strict punishments for those who wouldn't comply with the newly imposed Islamic laws. That wasn't just it. The change in the country was severe for men as well. A man couldn't go outside and walk in the streets if he was wearing a t-shirt with short sleeves. Men and women who were not married or related to one another could not be seen in public at all. During this time, we used to live in the countryside where the people weren't as open-minded and educated as in the big cities, like Tehran. It was easy for these people to be swayed by the new rigid pro-Islamic laws that the regime was slowly introducing. The country and everyone in it had drastically changed!

After the revolution, the country was standing on the

precipice of massive destruction. I was 14 when Saddam Hussein of Iraq attacked Iran on September 22, 1980, with all his might and power. That was the beginning of a chapter that would eventually be considered as the darkest phase in Iranian history. Millions of lives were lost, countless homes were destroyed, and the country was left in ruins. The images of war-torn Iran are still fresh in my memory. I can never forget the misery and depression people went through. Some say, almost the entire young generation was annihilated. Only aged people were seen walking the streets.

I'll go ahead and be honest with you. Subconsciously, I was looking for trouble all my childhood. I don't know why I wanted to put myself in a dangerous situation. I think it was an attempt to seek attention. I guess me stealing money from my father's wallet and then from the pillowcase was just a preview of the risk I was now going to take. Seeking trouble had become a habit of mine. I distinctly remember the bodies being brought home from the war front. I saw the coffins laden with flowers and how people were crying over the dead and praising them and celebrating the martyrs. Women were wailing and beating their chests and heads out of deep sorrow. A part of me envied the love and attention the fallen soldiers were being given. That was the kind of love and care I craved for myself, but I felt I wasn't good enough to deserve all that. After all, that was how my life had treated me. I fantasized that someday I too could be a hero, and people would come and cry over my dead body.

I was young and filled with youthful energy and determination. Serving in war seemed like a perfect way to earn respect and glory. And also an ideal way to escape from the life that had given me nothing but pain and suffering. Back then, I had started going to a mosque almost every day. There, they preached me about Islam and how I was supposed to fight for it. That's where I was brainwashed to join the Army and blow myself up in the mines. It was long sessions of brainwashing that convinced me to blow myself up on the battlefield. They preached me and others like me three things. First, your family will be happy and proud to have seen you serving your country and religion. Second, you will be mourned and grieved by the nation. And third, you will go to heaven where you will get 72 virgins. That was very tempting for me. Above all else, volunteering to fight seemed like an easy way to get the attention that I never got in my life. As a result, my three friends and I went and volunteered to join the armed forces. I was ready to go and fight and die. Nobody could stop me from going to the war, not even my family.

Nosrat and my father tried to bring me back to my senses.

But I had made up my mind. There was no turning back for me. When the news reached Shiraz, Zahra, my mother, and my uncles they also expressed their discontent over my decision. Still, my answer was the same, *"I am going to fight for God and my country. I will return as a hero or a martyr."* My family tried to talk some sense into me. They reminded me I was only 14. I was just a boy, and boys don't go to war. But nothing affected me. I didn't care if my neighbor's husband died in the war or if it was a family friend whose body was ripped into pieces on the battlefield. All I knew was that I'd go to heaven. So even if I die, what's wrong with that? That wasn't me. That was the brainwashing speaking.

I wanted to become a suicide bomber and blow myself up. I was so damaged at the time that I was ready to blow myself up into pieces. I was sick and tired of my dysfunctional life. I was fascinated by this proposition, even though I didn't know anything about fighting in a war.

My family couldn't change my mind. They had to give in to my stubbornness. I remember I was the happiest person in my village on the day I was to leave for my military training. I was waiting for the day to arrive impatiently. I was extremely eager to leave behind everything that had hurt me. My friend's brother drove my friends and me to the base. Before we left, our families bid us farewell, and we kissed the Quran for blessings.

The days I spent at the base was an entirely new experience for me. I hadn't lived a life like this before. Almost everything that happened over there was new to me. I went through three months of training. At the training camp, I used to observe the faces of other soldiers. Some of them looked excited, while others looked confused.

As for me, I was feeling mixed emotions. I was nervous but also eager to find out what happens next. All the trainees were often abruptly awakened at five in the morning with urgent shouts of "Go! Go! Go!" Sometimes the smoke was thrown into the barrack rooms to add to the realism. Many of my fellow trainees were young teenage boys like me, and we were taught how to shoot and dismantle landmines. We were taught how to kill. I couldn't imagine how it would feel like to take someone's life. It was both scary and exciting. The training period was strict and rigorous. We were forced to wake up as early as 4:00 am and ordered to run the length of the entire compound where the training was conducted. That was just the warm-up session, which was followed by grueling sets of pushups and exercises in muddy ditches. There were times I couldn't keep up with other child soldiers. I had no idea that physical training would be so exhausting. It made me regret my decision to join the army. When we were made to crawl in the narrow and dirty ditches, my elbows got scratched. When they used to throw gas grenades in barracks during the drill, I couldn't breathe. Besides all that, the military used to rouse patriotic emotions in us by lecturing us on the value of Islamic jihad and its benefits. They kept on promising us heaven after martyrdom. They made us wear keys around our necks, telling us that it was our key to unlock the door to paradise after we die fighting for Iran and Islam.

Three months flew by, and I didn't even realize it. In the meantime, the war had gotten more intense. When the training was over, we were sent to the frontlines close to the Iraqi border. There were many kinds of bombs, including chemical ones, and I suffered from the damage inflicted by the chemicals. Once, there was an attack at two o'clock in the morning, and bullets were whistling all around. It was utterly chaotic, and I saw soldiers dying left and right. I was scared, and I knew that I was going to die, and I didn't know what to do. But I still had my pride and was too afraid to say, *"I don't want to do this."* The bodies were strewn everywhere. Some soldiers were missing an arm, some were missing a leg, and some were lying dead on the battlefield with half of their faces blown off. After the attack and even after witnessing the bodies covered in blood and gore, there were young boys, aged 13 to 16, who were just excited to be part of something meaningful and significant. That incident was the first shock that came to me, but somehow I tried to digest the horror that I had just seen with my naked eyes.

Then the worst day of my life came. It's the day embedded in my mind. Several of us were sent out to dismantle landmines, and two of my friends were strolling ahead of me. The next thing I remember is mines exploding all around us, and bullets flying everywhere. I was terrified. The only thing I could hear was frantic cries of *"Allahu Akbar," "Allahu Akbar," "Allahu Akbar"* as the bullets pierced through the flesh, and the landmines blew body parts.

Everything was happening so fast. It was as if the world was coming to an end. Suddenly, one friend of mine dropped like a rock to the ground and didn't move. I stood motionless, stunned, staring at his lifeless body and slowly realizing that he had been shot in the head. I had already seen many people die, but this was different. He was my friend. He was just a kid, like me. And now he was dead. The landmines were exploding, the bullets were being fired, and the air was filled with dust and smoke. Bodies were being blown into pieces. My friends were taking their last breaths in front of me, and all I could hear were the earsplitting sounds of explosions and firing, and the soldiers crying in pain. It was in that moment I began to realize I was just one of the many child soldiers the Iranian regime had brainwashed and recruited to serve as foot soldiers. Suddenly, I realized I couldn't go through with the mission I had volunteered for. Suddenly, I knew I didn't want to die. But I couldn't go and say that I'm sorry I can't go on with the mission. My hopes of becoming a hero and having people cry over my grave were gone. The only thing in my mind was that I did not want to die like this.

That was wrong. Somehow I could see how children were tricked into becoming child soldiers. What did we know about weapons? What did we know about fighting? I needed to find a way to escape all of it. I felt desperation and panic, and I needed a plan to stay alive. But there was no time to plan. No place to run! There was an explosion near me that threw me a couple of meters away. I wasn't hurt, but my head was spinning, and my vision was compromised. I could hear a whizzing sound in my ears, as I tried to stand up on my feet.

What I did next was not something I had ever thought of doing before. The idea came to me in a moment, and I didn't waste another minute to give it a second thought. I just acted on an impulse. I thought if I got wounded, no one would expect me to stay on the battlefield. If I got injured, I would stay alive. That was my only way out, and I needed to act on it right away. Without allowing myself any time to think, I took my Kalashnikov and put its muzzle to the lower part of the inside of my left arm and pulled the trigger with my right hand. I fired a single shot. It was an experience I wouldn't wish for anybody. I will never forget the unbearable pain. I waited for help to come. The blood was gushing out from my arm, and the pain was so severe that I can feel the waves of it while writing this passage. Soldiers rushed to my help and wrapped me in a blanket. They took me away from the warzone.

I was brought to a camp where other soldiers and child soldiers were taking their last breaths. Some were shot in the eye, and some were shot in the throat. There was blood everywhere. It was just chaos. Those who rushed to my help were trying to stop the bleeding, but my veins were bleeding excessively. I was gaining and losing consciousness repeatedly. The next thing I remember is being carried away in the back of a tank with other wounded soldiers. I was taken to a base from where a chopper flew me to Shiraz, not by choice, but because it was the nearest city. All in all, it was a nightmare through and through. Shivers run down my spine even today when I recall that day. I spent a few days in a hospital in Shiraz, and then I was taken to a bigger and better hospital in Esfahan. The pain wouldn't go away. Even if I was conscious, I felt like the pain would make me faint. A surgery was performed on my arm to fix the damaged veins. The surgical operation was successful, but the recovery was long and painful. I got 65 stitches. The injury was so severe that despite attending physiotherapy sessions, I feel discomfort in my left arm to this day. While I was in Shiraz, my mother, Zahra, and her family looked after me. My mother especially went above and beyond the call of duty to give me comfort. She didn't sleep for several nights, trying to look after me.

For her, I was a hero, which was very unsettling for me. The same was the case with my father. Everyone looked at me proudly. I was a hero in their eyes. That further made me feel ashamed and guilty because deep down, I knew what I had done. I had shot myself, and everyone thought I was shot in the war. I couldn't escape the feeling that I was a loser, a coward, who doesn't deserve all the respect and adoration I was getting. I was not brave. I was a liar.

I didn't even know the real reason why the war broke out. Years later, I came to see that it was because of Khomeini who wanted to get other Islamic countries to become Shia Muslim nations. For that, he was using the Iranian government, youth, and children, sacrificing them to fulfill his agenda. To accomplish his goal, he was brainwashing kids to join the Army. Today, I thank God for opening my eyes before going through the mission.

Finding out about my mother had made me feel abandoned and unwanted. Being forcefully violated by a man in a truck had made me feel dirty and humiliated. Getting beaten by a man I looked up to had made me feel confused and betrayed. Now, I had to carry the horrible secret that I had shot myself with my rifle to avoid fighting honorably like a man. That made me feel mortified and worthless. This wave of guilt and shame that struck me made me hate myself more than ever.

Of course, I kept the big secret to myself. I didn't tell the truth to anyone. This was another secret I had to keep to myself. Even to this day, my family doesn't know what I did to escape from the battlefield. Years later, I told my son that I shot myself. I wasn't a hero. I had to let the secret out of my system. Doing so made me feel better.

If you think that was it, you are dead wrong. There was more guilt, remorse, sadness, and loneliness to come in my life that made me weaker than I ever was. The next phase in my life was connected to the horrendous events I had lived through in the past.

Living in post-revolution Iran was not easy for anyone.

There were restrictions on living your life freely. You could not drink, you could not court women, and you could not get your hands on any form of media that wasn't filtered. After I recovered from my terrible physical wound, I went through the second round of depression. I couldn't understand the purpose of my life. I was a wholly lost man with fake honor to his credit. The fact that I performed a cowardly act to avoid combat in the war, shattered me even more. I knew what the regime did with child soldiers was wrong, but now I was living the life of a coward, which was rather disturbing for me. As a result, I barely got out of bed. I lost my appetite and grew weaker and weaker. I wasn't interested in doing anything. My life was a mess already, and now there were these images from the war that kept haunting me.

I used to have nightmares. The worst of them was the one where someone was shooting my friends point-blank in the heads, right in front of me. And just when this unidentified soldier was about to kill me, I used to wake up, covered in sweat and panting.

A few months later, when I could manage to do some work, my father insisted on meeting some of my cousins in Esfahan and starting work with them. I was reluctant to meet anyone new, and the war wasn't over yet, I was baffled. It seemed as if I was incapable of making the right decisions in my life. Every decision that I made fell flat on its face. First, it was the decision to accept Ali as my mentor, then the decision to travel to Abadan all alone, and then the decision to volunteer in the war. I was making mistakes after mistakes for which I had to pay.

When I couldn't find an alternative, I got in touch with my cousins and started working with them in Esfahan. My cousins were older than me. They were fun-loving and upbeat. In the beginning, I was reclusive and didn't prefer to blend in with them. But after a few weeks, I started spending more and more time with them. We used to go out together, eat dinner together, and even drink together.

Yes. You heard me right. My cousins introduced me to *liquor*. At first, when they offered me, I resisted, as a true Muslim should, but soon I gave in to my temptation. The next time I saw them drinking, I joined them for a glass or two. It was quite a challenge to buy alcohol in post-revolution Iran. The extremist regime sealed all the pubs and bars, so we had to purchase liquor illegally from a few hidden spots and make sure we didn't get caught. There was no chance of drinking in public, so we used to bring alcohol to our home and drink at night. We even had to be careful about disposing of the empty bottles.

My cousins drank for fun and pleasure, while I took casual drinking to a whole other level. I never realized I was walking on the path of substance abuse. Alcohol took my mind off things that disturbed me. Things I wanted to forget. Things I wanted to leave behind. And I liked that. I had no idea at the time how much my decision to drink would affect my life. All I knew was that it made me feel better for a little while and at least temporarily erased my feelings of guilt and inadequacy. But I was so wrong. If truth be told, my real destruction, the destruction of my physical being, had just begun.

Chapter 3
My Life after the War

"I don't fear death so much as I fear its prologues: loneliness, decrepitude, pain, debilitation, depression, senility. After a few years of those, I imagine death presents like a holiday at the beach."–**Mary Roach**

The phases a person goes through in a troubled life are indeed more painful than death. Phases like loneliness, hopelessness, senility, and depression suck the life out of the human body to the extent that one can't help but consider ending his life. After befriending my cousins and joining them in their business in Esfahan, I discovered myself again. I was still young, but I felt like a grown-up. I was helping my cousins run their business, and I was drinking.

And the best part was that it was helping me get through the catastrophe that my life was. It was like I had gained a superpower that allowed me to forget everything that I wanted to leave behind. All the bad things that had happened to me, all the events that had tortured me, and all the experiences that had disturbed me, I could put them behind if I wanted by drinking. *It was that easy*, I thought. Finally, I had figured out a way to put my mind at ease.

How could something that relaxes you and soothes down your worries be bad? I thought. I did not even realize when exactly my occasional drinking turned into a habit. Little did I know that my drinking habit would become the addiction that would make me regret the day I accepted the offer to join my cousins and have a drink with them.

In case you are wondering what happened to the war, it was still waging on, and thousands of men were dying. Khomeini wasn't backing out, and soldiers were dying. Men and children were dying. Whenever I heard about someone's child being martyred in the war, the horrific images of the war ran before my eyes. The cries, the blood, the gore, the bombs, and the bullets, none of those things had escaped my mind. I could only imagine what this kid must have experienced in the war, and how terrified he would have become when he saw the brutality and ruthlessness of fighting. Thinking about how scared he must be on the battlefield just before he died bothered me and left me disturbed beyond measure.

Despite the turmoil in the country, my visits to Shiraz were as frequent as they were before the war started. As I said, that was the only thing that offered me solace in difficult times. I knew if I go to Shiraz to my mother's family, I would feel better. Some things kept me interested there. My uncles valued me, and I loved traveling in Shiraz with them. And of course, my mother was there. I enjoyed spending time with her. But there was something else that had tickled my fancy in Shiraz lately. Out of my three uncles, the middle one had recently got divorced. He had two sons from his previous marriage. After some time, he ended up marrying another woman. This woman had three daughters of her own, three beautiful daughters. After recovering from my self-inflicted injury, whenever I visited Shiraz, I used to hang around with my uncle's stepdaughters a lot. I remember they were shy at first, but then they opened up when they got a little familiar with my face. They were honestly an excellent company to be with. Our friendship began with talking to each other, and then we started to make jokes, laugh, and play games. We were perfect together. My uncles used to take us out together to treat us, and I used to fancy those moments a lot.

Like I mentioned earlier, the village in Shiraz, where my mother lived, was a small village. The best thing about it was that you could get a tour of a lot of attractive sites on foot. You didn't have to own a car or drive one to explore the village. Thus, these three girls and I used to spend some quality time outside our house as well. Sometimes we would go to watch the movies, sometimes we would go out to eat ice cream, and sometimes we would go out and walk while talking to each other. It didn't take me long to realize that I had developed feelings for the second girl.

I liked talking to her. I think the thing that drew me close to her was her mindset. She used to think about what I used to think. She and I had almost the same opinions about everything that we saw, ate, or experienced. Time used to fly when talking to her. I felt comfortable when I was with her. But like any other teenage boy, I was afraid to say it to her. I didn't dare to admit that her innocence and simplicity smote me. I went through the same confusion and hesitation that every boy goes through when he falls in love with a girl for the first time. I couldn't express my appreciation and feelings for her no matter how much I wanted to, and how hard I tried. At least, I think, I decided to confess my love to her. That's what I remember.

The girl I was attracted to was kind, polite and affectionate to me. However, my only concern was that I didn't know if she liked me or not. She never gave me a sign if she was attracted to me, which confused me even more. What if I told her I liked her and she rejected me? That's the biggest fear of any man I suppose, and I was no different. And to be quite honest, I wasn't sure if I would be able to deal with rejection at that point in my life. That would be a little too much for me, so I decided to stay quiet. I didn't want to risk the relationship I had with her.

Also, I didn't want to admit it back then, but now when I think about it, I believe there was another reason why I buried my emotions for this girl deep in my heart. In my subconscious, I felt I was not worthy of her love and affection. I was a loser who lied to be a war hero; I was a rape victim, and recently, I had resorted to drinking so that I could escape from my past. Who I was and what happened with me somehow managed to stop me from expressing my feelings to this girl. I prefer to say that my dark side intervened with my noble intention of winning the affection of a young girl I had fallen in love with.

Whenever I used to leave Shiraz, I would say to myself that I would try confessing my love for her the next time I would visit. But that next time never came. I wasted all the time I had in mustering my confidence to say what I felt in my heart for her.

To this day, I consider that girl my first love. The girl to whom I couldn't say I love her. The girl I wanted to, but couldn't marry, because I was pushed into an arranged marriage with another girl.

People in Iran get married at a young age. It wasn't like

that always, but after the Islamic revolution, getting married at a young age became a cultural norm. That was the case because dating wasn't allowed in post-revolution Iran. Men and women were not supposed to be seen in each other's company unless they were blood related or married.

When I turned 15, my family decided it was time for me to get married. My aunt said she knew the family of a girl named Mehry, and that I should go and see her. Although I couldn't stop thinking about my uncle's stepdaughter, I knew getting married to her was not possible. I wasn't confident enough to ask her hand in marriage. Thus, I agreed to see this girl. One day when I visited her place with my family, I found she wasn't exactly unattractive. However, there was something about her that didn't appeal to me. If truth be told, my marriage with Mehry was almost decided. I was just asked to look at her so that I know who I was getting married to. I remember my cousins telling me that when it came to arranged marriages, it didn't matter what's presented to you, as long as you got laid. That made sense to my adolescent hormones.

On top of everything, I was told by the adults of my family that arranged marriages weren't that bad. People who marry strangers eventually come to like each other with time. Thus, I said "yes," and I was considered to be engaged to

Mehry. Over the next couple of months, her family occasionally brought her to visit me, or sometimes my family took me to her place. There were family members present, and we were never alone. So, I never had time to ask what she felt about this arrangement; to ask what her opinion was about this marriage.

I passively went along with the idea of being engaged to Mehry because that was expected of me, and it would have been quite challenging to rebel against those expectations. However, when I thought of the love of my life, and whenever her face popped into my mind, I felt I was making the wrong decision. I was betraying Mehry by not telling her the truth. The truth was there was nothing wrong with her. I just realized I didn't love her. But there was nothing that I could do now. If I announced that I wanted to end the engagement and didn't want to marry Mehry, then that would damage her reputation and bring shame to her family. It was like I was caught in the hell of my own making. *I should have said and done something before the engagement*, I thought. However, it was too late.

There were times when I thought I was getting married to make my family and relatives happy, instead of myself. Nobody seemed to care about me nor understand my feelings. Nobody cared about how I felt. I was carrying all that emotional baggage and all that damage. I didn't know what to do. I was paralyzed to the point where I had no energy to fight. So I married Mehry, hoping I would soon fall in love with her.

The wedding ceremony was a private affair through and through. It was quiet and straightforward, and no one outside of Mehry's and my family was invited except for a few close friends. The news of me getting married had reached Shiraz, and whenever I thought of that, I felt sad. What if my uncle's stepdaughter had the same feelings for me as I had for her? What must she have gone through after coming to know that I was getting married to someone else? These thoughts bothered me a lot.

Everyone who attended my wedding wished Mehry and me all the happiness in the world. I guess everyone at my wedding was happy except me.

My life after marriage changed utterly. I had the responsibility of my wife now. It wasn't just me anymore. I had to think of Mehry as well before making any decision. I wanted to be a good husband. Although I was very young to call myself a husband, I tried my best to fit into the role of a loving and caring husband. As for Mehry, she was good to me too. Sometimes I wondered how she would feel if I told her that I was in love with another girl and that I didn't want to marry her in the first place. She was young like me, and she didn't deserve to be left heartbroken in such a young age, so I never opened my mouth. I also never asked her if she was ready to marry me because her parents said she should. If she said yes, then that would have unsettled me more because I thought of ditching the whole idea of getting married to her, a thousand times at least.

As a wife, Mehry was obedient. She was a perfect wife for an Iranian man. She would do what I asked her to do. She would put my comfort before her own. When I returned home after spending the entire day outside, she used to keep dinner ready, knowing that I would be hungry. Now, even though I wasn't delighted with the decision that I had made under pressure, I wasn't absolved of my marital duties, and neither was Mehry. I was reluctant to start a family at this point in my life, but I guess that's what happens when you get married young. You become a young parent. And that's what happened to me as well.

My eldest son was born almost after one year of marriage. That made me a 16-year-old father. Yes, that's how young I was at the time. But anyway, that kind of thing is common in Iran even today, so people don't mind if you become a father while other boys your age are still going to school. It's funny, but it's true.

Both Mehry's and my family were quite happy. I had become a father at such a young age, and our parents had become grandparents at a young age as well. For me, it was as if life was going too fast. It was kind of scary as well. If I told anyone abroad that I got married when I was 15, and I had my first baby when I was 16, I think they would faint. But that's how life in Iran used to be.

My parental duties did not come to an end with just one baby. About a year and a half later, Mehry and I had a second son.

My marriage to Mehry didn't make me stop drinking. I drank when I had to. I couldn't go on living with the past that tortured me more than anything. Whenever I was alone, my head got filled with disturbing images from the war and my childhood. My past never stopped following me. And the only way I could soothe its effect on me was by drinking. Mehry tried to stop me from drinking when she saw it had become my habit, but that wasn't enough for me. My thirst for alcohol was far more intense than anyone could imagine. It wasn't like I used to stay drunk all the time. But when I felt the urge to drink, it was difficult for me to stop.

Similarly, when I sat with my friends and cousins, I often

returned home drunk. However, I never used to drink whenever I visited Shiraz. Even after getting married, when I took Mehry and my kids to visit my mother and my uncles in Shiraz, I chose to stay sober.

I started to believe this is how the rest of my life would pass. Every evening I would return home to Mehry, waiting for me with our two sons and my haunting memories chasing me like demons. But I was wrong. Fate had decided something else for me.

My father was still running his trucking business. His 18-wheeler was hauling powdered cement from one city to another. I remember my brother, who was still working for my father, was out of town on vacation, and my father's trailer had some mechanical problems. Thus, my father had to ask one of his friends, who was also in the trucking business and had just bought a brand new 18-wheeler trailer, if he could borrow his van to transport 24-ton cement load to Yazd.

A man named Mohammed was to drive the trailer. He wasn't experienced enough to drive a rig of this type, so my father asked me to go with him on the trip to make sure the job is completed correctly. I helped Mohammed load the cement, which was a tiring job, and soon we were on our way to Yazd. Mohammed's business partner was with us on the trip. The trip was a nice change since it was a long time I had hit the road. Since Mohammed was driving the trailer, his partner and I got along well. We talked about the war and how it showed no signs of ending any time soon. We talked about the revolution and how it changed Iran. It was nice talking to him because his opinions on the war and revolution were almost the same as mine. Mohammed's partner was sitting in the front seat, and both of us wouldn't stop talking.

At some point, I noticed that Mohammed was continually using the trailer's air brakes when he wanted to slow down, instead of downshifting. Although I had zero experience when it came to driving 18-wheeler trailers, I felt Mohammed should have used the gears and not just the brakes. I thought I should ask him why he was doing that, but I got busy talking again, and it slipped my mind.

Mohammed's partner was telling me about his kids and how much he loved them when suddenly the brake system ran out of air, and Mohammed lost control of the trailer. The oncoming vehicles were frantically trying to avoid our careening rig and its 24-ton load. Mohammed tried to pull on the emergency brakes and pressed on the brake pedal, but the trailer was entirely out of control. The next thing I remember is that the trailer lost balance and flipped several times on the highway.

I passed out, and to this day, I have no clear memory of what precisely happened next. I remember when I regained consciousness, I was stuck under heavy metal, and it was pressing against my chest so hard that I could barely draw a breath. On top of that, my right hand was severely burned. I couldn't see it because I was under the metal of the trailer. As I was lying there, the only thing in my mind was that I was going to die. I was almost certain. As I continued to gasp for air, I thought to myself that this was the day when Mehry would become a young widow, and my sons would become orphans. The only word I could hear was the partner taking Mohammad's name again and again.

I looked over and saw Mohammed, and realized that his situation was at least as bad as mine. He was trapped in the upside-down trailer and unable to move, but he was still able to talk. He asked me to tell his family that he loved them, and I asked him to pass on the same message to my kids.

I don't remember when the help came. I woke up in the hospital several hours later. I don't know how the people who came to help us were able to pull us out of the wreck. It was in the hospital when they told me that the trailer had crashed about two or three hundred meters off the highway. The hospital staff gave me the news that Mohammed's partner had broken his legs, but he survived. However, by the time people were able to pull Mohammed out, he was already dead.

It took me three weeks to recover. Once I could stand on my feet, I visited the garage and saw the wreckage of the trailer. One look at it and I thought, how did I even survive that. I was amazed that none of my bones were broken, but the severe burn on my right hand left scars I will always have. It indeed was a miracle that I was standing there alive; I was utterly awestruck.

Chapter 4
An Unexpected Journey

"I've learned that fear limits you and your vision. It serves as blinders to what may be just a few steps down the road for you. The journey is valuable, but believing in your talents, your abilities, and your self-worth can empower you to walk down an even brighter path. Transforming fear into freedom - how great is that?" – **Soledad O'Brien**

After all the tragic episodes I had been through in life, I was surely blinded by fear. The element of doubt in my life was like blinders, obstructing my view of what was coming up next. But I guess that doesn't stop the world from spinning. I think that doesn't warrant you to stop living as well. You have to continue living. No matter how difficult it gets for you.

After recovering from the horrific trailer accident, I had another personal turmoil to recover from. Mohammad, the guy who was driving the truck one minute, was dead the other minute. It was disconcerting. That's how unexpected death is. I guess I was reminded of this fact again. The first time I came across this harsh and bitter reality was when I saw my friends dropping dead on the battlefield in the war.

Would my life be normal ever again? I used to think. Would I ever feel happy again? I guess I had no answers to those questions. These questions just fueled my grief. And the only way I could tackle my pain was by numbing my senses by drinking. The sad part of my life was that I didn't feel happy when I looked at my family around me. Nothing could give me pleasure. My wife and my two sons were there, but I just wasn't moved by their presence. They weren't enough to make me forget my past. Now that I think about it, I realize maybe the way I felt back then was one of the side effects of getting married and parenting two kids at such an early age. Or perhaps, it was just my demons that continued to haunt me relentlessly.

Mehry used to talk to me, and I used to speak to her back. But that didn't ease the survivor's guilt I was experiencing. The fact that I lived and Mohammad died was challenging to accept. The fact that I managed to get out of the war alive, and my friends could not was difficult to accept. There wasn't a day that passed without me thinking about my friends that I lost in the war. We went off to the war so excited, and in just a few days' time, we were left with no hope and shattered souls.

Every night when I was lying in bed, I used to think what my purpose was in life? Why was I even alive? Was my life heading in the right direction? The more I thought about those things, the more depressed I became. I wish someone could have told me that things would become worse for you, but in the end, you will understand the purpose of your life that you so passionately seek. I wish someone would have told me that the road you are walking might seem self-destructive, but one day you will come to understand the reason why you walked that road in the first place. I wanted someone to tell me that the path I was on would not lead to my end. There is light at the end of the tunnel, even if I cannot see it at the moment.

The next chapter of my life begins about six months after the trailer accident. I realized that the Iranian government had arranged to send some of the soldiers, who had been injured in the war along with their families, out of the country. The government had made arrangements for several hundred people to migrate to Damascus, Syria, for the time being. At first, I felt relieved that a little change would do me right. However, little did I know that this wasn't a kind of vacation I was hoping for. That was more of a religious therapy for the wounded soldiers and families who had lost their loved ones in the war. I had no idea how this cross-country experience would turn out for me.

When I was made aware of this arrangement, I felt

thrilled. I wanted to find a way to get out of my situation and not look back on my past life. And I thought this was the chance I was waiting for. Perhaps this could take me far from the life I was living. I wanted to escape the feelings of shame and worthlessness that had sort of chained my feet. My only mistake was to believe that the Iranian government had something positive planned for us that would release me from the clutches of the war. But sadly, that wasn't the case. It was not a paid vacation.

I wasn't feeling bad about leaving Mehry and my two sons behind. It wasn't like I was going for years. It was a program that would last for a few months, and then I was expected to return to Iran back to my family. So I said goodbye to my family, kissed my sons, and off I went to Syria, a country I had never been to.

My father dropped me to the airport. Till then, I was fine. The first bolt of lightning struck me when I boarded the plane. The moment I sat in that plane, my guilt and shame overtook me once I realized I was sitting amidst real war heroes. The mothers in the aircraft had lost their sons and husbands, and the soldiers were actually brave enough to fight in the war. As for me, I was a fake, wounded soldier. I was perhaps the only one who chickened out on the battlefield and decided to shoot myself, so I could get rid of the war. If truth be told, I didn't even belong there in that plane. The moment I realized that I felt like jumping off the plane. How would I talk to other people? How would I look at other soldiers in the eye and tell what happened to me? How would I live with all these people for the next few months?

During the flight to Damascus, Syria, it dawned upon me that this trip wasn't what I expected it to be. It was something else, and it would be hard on my nerves to get through this. How will I ever make it to the end of this program? I asked myself, and without any exaggeration, I had no answer to that question. I felt everything inside me was going to explode. I was not sure how I was managing a calm exterior. Behaving normally on the trip was one of the hardest things I have ever had to do. I was not sure how much longer I could bear all of it. Here, I was a liar and a coward among all the heroes who deserved the praise they were getting. I was amidst all those who had died for what they believed in. I was someone who had deliberately injured himself so that he could be sent home. There was no one that I could talk to about my feelings, let alone discuss my terrible secret with them.

Syria was a lot different to my eyes. Of course, I had never traveled to any other country before; but still, Syria was different in many ways. The houses, the streets, and the mosques, everything was different. The architecture of the mosques was pretty different, except for the ones that were built by Iranians. The weather, however, was similar to Iran, but the country was less green. I could only imagine how good it would have been if I had come to Damascus on vacation.

The hotel that was arranged for us was not a five-star one. It was a moderate hotel with simple rooms and amenities. But that was not my concern at the time. I was worried about more important things, like how would I make it to the end of this program, and how would I hide my guilt and shame as long as I was here? I felt trapped. I didn't know where to go. I just wanted to go far from here as well. As soon as we checked into the hotel, I had the overwhelming urge to be alone, so I headed out for a walk, thinking that it might help me lose some of the pent up emotions. I wandered around aimlessly for what seemed to be a long time. I had no destination in my mind, I was in a new city, and all I wanted was to be far away from it and never look back on it again. I walked on the sidewalks, I walked in the narrow streets of the city, and I looked into the shops. It was my first day in the city, and I was trying to find ways to kill time. How sad was I?

As I was wandering around, thinking about my life, I came across a bar. As soon as I saw the bar, I knew I should not go inside. With the type of emotional turmoil I was in, I knew I would end up doing something I would regret. I turned away from there and came back to the hotel. But I knew that the thought of what I discovered in the streets of Damascus was not going to leave me alone. I knew, sooner or later, I would end up going there. It was only a matter of time that I would find myself craving to get drunk. I felt relieved that Syria was brave enough to have bars in the corner of the streets where men like me could drink to forget their losses, grieves, and sorrows. *The program I was attending was more of a religious therapy, as I mentioned before. As if they hadn't done enough brainwashing already. For me, it was somewhat difficult to bear it. Each day was a solemn occasion. It started with many prayers and ended on a variety of religious observances. I was so not looking forward to a religious congregation. I was being forced to be a part of it.* A week into the program, and I had it up to my neck. I couldn't take it anymore. I decided I had to do myself a favor and gulp down a few glasses of alcohol, as soon as possible. I couldn't breathe among people who were so devoted to their religion even after the war. Some mothers had lost their only sons. There were widows left with young children to feed because their husbands went off to the war and never came back. Some soldiers had returned from the war with amputated legs and arms. But all of them were still pious Muslims. They loved God even after losing so much in the name of God. For them, life was all about religion. It was all about Islam and being Muslim.

On the other hand, I wasn't like that. I wasn't even remotely like that. I wasn't praying at all. I had started to believe that God was someone who abandons you when you need him the most. I didn't even believe in the cause after witnessing the atrocities with child soldiers in the war. Seeing all of that changed my perspective. I was drinking, and I was smoking opium whenever I could. And I was into another shady business. Since my father had the trailer, so I traveled from one city to another, smuggling opium and VHS videos and selling them in Esfahan at such a young age. That was after the war took place. In short, I was nothing like them. I couldn't find the courage to praise the Lord, who had forgotten about me in the first place. I started to feel suffocated amidst all these people who were conservative and religious, but supposedly better than me. I felt ashamed and asked myself, what am I doing here? I didn't belong there. I was such a misfit. However, I had learned how to safeguard my secrets. I hid my identity from everyone. I didn't even utter a word about how my faith in God had started to evaporate. When it was time to attend the religious meetings every day, I made excuses to participate in those activities, which were mostly lectures on Islam, Khomeini, and Holy Prophets. I told others I wasn't feeling well.

I was with strange people and hadn't had a drop of alcohol or a puff of opium for some time. I was craving for some. I knew this phase would come over me in a few days, especially since I saw that bar. One day I skipped a session I was supposed to attend and went out for a walk. I tried not to think of it, but I knew where my steps were headed to. I knew I was walking in the direction of that bar I saw the other day. And after a few minutes, I was there. I went inside and got hammered. I drank as if it was the last day of my life. I drank as if my life depended on it. I was drunk and arguing with the people seated around me in the bar in no time at all. I don't exactly remember what I was debating about and who I was arguing with because I was intoxicated by the time. It was the only way I knew how to drown my emotions. As the argument proceeded, I got very loud and disruptive, so someone called in the police, and I was taken to the police station. There was a lot of confusion because I did not speak Arabic. Since it was an official matter, the situation could not be resolved without calling in a translator.

When the police found out where I was staying, they called for someone from the group to come and get me because I was in no condition to go back to the hotel on my own. The matter could not have gotten any worse. I was caught, and my secret was out. I knew everyone would know about me that I was a drunkard. Had I known the real purpose of this trip was, I wouldn't have come with this group. Signing up to join this program to escape the clichés of my mundane and depressing life was the biggest mistake I ever made. The whole plan of having some time to myself alone in a foreign country kind of blew up in my face, and now I had to face the consequences.

The next morning, I was questioned by the leaders of the organization I had come to Damascus with. I tried my very best to justify the situation, but the events of the last night were not in my favor. In my defense, I started by denying that I was drunk at all, which did not work for very long, obviously, so I admitted that I was drunk. The situation was difficult as I was an Iranian soldier on a semi-official visit to a foreign country, and my conduct was not representative of a war veteran. The whole situation was further exacerbated by the fact that I was there on a religious trip. During the questioning, I was asked things I never expected I would be asked. They asked me what convinced me to drink, and how much did I drink. They asked me since when did I start drinking, and whether I enjoyed knocking myself out. The whole time, I wanted to melt with guilt and disappear into the floor. I felt like everyone was looking at me and judging me, and I wanted to get as far away from them as possible. That was the only thing on my mind at that time. I wanted to get out of there.

I knew I was not a good influence on those around me, and I did not want people looking at me with disgust and hatred. I was deeply saddened by the fact that no one thought about what I might have gone through to become like this. No one bothered to empathize with me. They all just went ahead and judged me. There is a reason that a person becomes self-destructive. There's a story behind an individual who commits to alcoholism. But no one was ready to understand that. Like most of my life, in this situation as well, no one thought about me.

At the end of the interrogation, they told me they had to send my file to Tehran to make a decision. They hated me for who I was. The new Iran, under Khomeini's iron-fisted reign, was not ready to accept an alcoholic that easily. Drinking was simply unpardonable. I knew they would either put me in jail or flog me or send me for some therapy. I knew something terrible and ruthless awaited me once my file was reviewed in Tehran. I was sent back to Iran immediately. They made it clear that they didn't want me there. There was no time for me to stay in Iran and wait for the punishment they were going to give me. Under Islamic law, I was nothing more than a bad influence, a termite who would infect other people as well. Thus, before the government could arrest me and make an example out of me for other men who were fond of drinking, I had to get out of there without wasting time.

I made the necessary arrangements with the help of my close friend. Before I could even prepare myself for another journey, I decided to leave Iran for Istanbul, Turkey. I couldn't take Mehry and my sons with me because I didn't have that much money. I barely stayed in Iran to sell the land and the car that my father had given me because the authorities could come and have me arrested any day. Escaping Iran like that was something I had never imagined in my wildest dream. I could not even believe what was happening. Suddenly, my life was going way too fast.

My eldest son was two years old, and the second one was of six months at the time. I didn't know if what I was doing was for the good or not. I didn't even know when I would be able to see my family again. But the reality was I could not exist in Iran anymore. I had to get out of there. I felt I would lose my mind if I had to stay there any longer. I just took this opportunity and escaped from Iran and told my family that I was going to *Mashad*, a holy city in Iran, for prayers. I didn't tell anyone where I was going.

What exactly did I have in mind when I left Iran? Why was I running like a fugitive from my home country? When I try to recall those details, nothing comes to my mind. It seems that my emotions and sentiments from the time I was eloping have faded over time. But given the circumstances I was living in, I like to believe I was relieved.

After everything I had suffered in Iran, I thought that getting out of that country might help me gain control of my emotions. I felt that it would help me learn a little perspective. I felt that leaving Iran would let me figure out what I wanted to do in my life, and how to gain control of my life. The best plan that I could come up with for leaving Iran was going to West Germany and seeking asylum as a refugee.

It seemed like a great plan at the time. But it wasn't easy for me to buy a ticket and catch the next flight to West Germany. Of course, I had to take the tougher route. I collected as much money as I could within one week and bought a bus ticket to Istanbul, Turkey. I had decided I wanted to leave, and I wanted to go as quickly as I could before anything else could happen that would derail my plans. It was a long journey to West Germany, and I was ready to make it.

After the debacle in Syria, I did not want to face my community any longer. I just wanted to go far away from this place where everyone seemed to know me and did not respect me. I just wanted to disappear. I wanted to go someplace where no one knew me. I felt like I had grown so sensitive that I could not take another person's judgment.

I was able to get a legitimate Iranian passport just in time. After making sure I had all the necessary documents that I would be needing for traveling abroad, I was off to Istanbul via bus. It was a few days' journey, and it was a somewhat uncomfortable one as well. As for my feelings, I guess they were mixed. I was going to be all alone there, which was a relief, but the same sense of impending loneliness was freaking me out a little. I knew myself well. I wasn't the very best version of myself when I was alone. You can consider the debacle in Syria as a reference here. I knew I gave in to my temptations rather quickly when I was alone.

The second thing that bothered me was my family. I was leaving behind my wife and sons for God knows how long.

It only occurred to me when I was hugging and kissing my sons and waving Mehry goodbye that I didn't have a clear plan ahead of me. I didn't know what would become of me once I left Iran. This thought frightened me. It made me feel vulnerable. And at the same time, it made me feel guilty for leaving my family behind with no hope of seeing them again. What was to become of Mehry in my absence? What was to become of my sons? I didn't have answers to those disturbing questions. On top of all that, they didn't know exactly where I was going and for how long.

The only plan I had was to reach West Germany, but my first destination was Istanbul, Turkey. From there, I would have to make efforts to leave for West Germany as soon as possible and register myself as a war refugee. And the chances were I would have to make it through East Germany to get to West Germany. It was a long journey ahead of me, and I had very limited resources to rely on.

I wish I could ask God for help for I knew the days ahead would be difficult. I wish I could say I trust in God, but when did God ever help me in my life? It seemed He had planned every single day of my life as an exam, a test that I barely managed to pass.

Chapter 5
My Journey to Turkey and Beyond

"I think our life is a journey, and we make mistakes, and it is how we learn from those mistakes and rebound from those mistakes that set us on the path that we're meant to be on."

– *Ellis Jay*

It was a long, exhausting, and tiring journey. I thought it would never come to an end. Even after crossing the Iranian-Turkish border, it was a long journey to Istanbul. I don't precisely remember the hours I spent sitting on the bus. As far as I remember, I slept through most of the journey. I was so worn out both mentally and physically that I felt I couldn't take another hour on the bus. All I remember is that the bus was passing a barren mountainous area of Orumiyeh, which meant we were getting close to the border.

It was early morning when the bus reached Istanbul. The sun was almost up when I caught the first glimpse of the city. The streets were crowded, and the marketplace was busy. People were getting out to start another day when I arrived in Istanbul. Istanbul, soaked in the golden hour of early morning sunlight, looked beautiful. I had read a lot about the city, its historical significance, and the culture over there. Still, a tired feeling weighed me down. I didn't exactly know what it was. Was it the tiredness from the journey? Was it my loneliness? Was it another bout of depression? I still hadn't quite figured it out. The first thing on my mind was to find a cheap place to stay. When I got off at the bus stop, I asked a few local people about the places I could stay. I didn't know the language, and it was tough. They told me something else, and I understood the opposite of it. It was good that I had slept on my journey to Istanbul. At least, I had the energy to walk in the unknown streets and look for a cheap place to crash in.

Staying at a hotel was out of the question. I couldn't afford a cheap hotel. What I was looking for was an accommodation, like a small room that I could rent. After much effort, I was able to find a place for accommodation in a narrow and somewhat downtrodden street. If truth be told, it was more of an alley rather than a road. However, the room I rented was small, clean, and cheap. It was quiet there. I guess that was the best thing about it.

Now, this was my chance to prove myself. I was allowed to do something productive in a country that was economically more stable than Iran at the time. There were endless opportunities here for me. But instead, I ended up wasting myself, just as I expected. Even if I wanted to get out and explore the city and figure out what would be the best thing for me to do, I stayed locked up in my room, drunk.

It was reasonably easy to buy alcohol in Istanbul. There was a small liquor store near the place where I lived, who was happy to deliver a bottle every day to my room. I was to run out of money soon if I continued wasting it on alcohol, but I was far from convincing myself to stop drinking. I don't know what I was trying to do. Was I trying to drink myself to death? Even if that thought crossed my mind, I wasn't bothered by it. I wanted to die and put an end to my miserable life that was heavily dominated by guilt and shame. Day after day after day, I stayed in my room and never stopped drinking. I was inebriated all the time. Memories flooded my mind. I couldn't stop pitying myself for all that happened to me, and I couldn't stop asking myself the same question: why did everything that happened to happen with me? Why me? Why was my childhood not normal? Why was I separated from my mother? Why was I assaulted? Why did I ever go to the war? Why did the accident happen? Why was I shamed publicly in Syria? There were too many reasons to drink.

On top of all that, I couldn't escape the thought of abandoning my family. I couldn't think of anything else but my family. I used to wake up thinking about my sons, and I used to go to sleep thinking about them. I couldn't help but feel guilty about what my sons would think of me when they grow up. They would hate me for abandoning them at such a young age. The fact that I could not see them anymore disturbed me a lot. I could hear voices in my head, telling me I was the worst father and husband in the world. While I was in Istanbul, every single day was the same for me. It started with the same feeling of guilt and ended with it as well. I couldn't care less if I ended up dead in that room. Someone would discover my body in a few days and would send it back to Iran. That would be better, I thought, because I had no strength to continue living my life without drinking. I had to drink as much as I could to bury my sorrows. I didn't want to get out of my room. I didn't want to go outside and meet people. All I wanted was to forget my past. But no matter how much I drank, my memories never left me alone. Even escaping from Iran didn't help me get rid of those disturbing memories.

I tried to convince myself by thinking maybe it was for the good that I left Iran and my boys. I would have been a bad influence on them, and they were better off without me. It was for their good. However, that consolation didn't work for very long. As soon as its effect began to wear off, I would find myself sitting in the corner of my room with a glass in my hand filled to the brim with alcohol. The undeniable fact I was trying to wrestle with in my mind was that I missed my sons. That's when I realized how much I loved them. Instead of standing up on my feet and doing something productive, I continued living in fear of moving ahead in life. I didn't shy away from calling myself a loser. I could have harnessed the love I felt for my kids to work toward improving my life and arranging for my sons to come over and live with me, but instead, I made that love my weakness. While the sun rose and set, I stayed in that godforsaken room slowly fading into oblivion. A month passed since I came to Istanbul, and it was time for me to get out of there. It turned out Turkey wasn't far enough to run away from all the guilt and shame I was trying to run away from. I was better off someplace really far. A place so far that my memories couldn't chase me anymore. I used to get out of my room to eat only. But the few acquaintances that I had made helped me buy a fake Turkish passport that would allow me to cross the border and escape to East Germany. Once I got my phony passport in my hand, I decided to leave and continue my journey.

 A few days in East Germany, and I knew I could not stay

there for long. Life in East Germany was tough. The hold of the ruling communist party, Socialist Unity Party of Germany, was strong, and that made life in East Germany entirely controlled and closely monitored. The communist authorities did not go easy on anyone they had doubts about. Luckily, I was very near to achieving my objective. All I had to do was cross the border that divided the country, and I would be in West Germany, just like I had planned. Thus, the next phase of my journey was becoming a stowaway. I stowed myself away in a railway baggage car that was leaving East Germany for West Germany. This way, I was able to reach West Germany overnight. Back in those days, a lot of people secretly fled East Germany and entered West Germany illegally. I tagged along with a group of similar people. These people warned me that it was a considerable risk, as doing so had resulted in the deaths of several escapees previously. Still, I had to get to West Germany as soon as possible, and this was the best way to cross the inner German border. If truth be told, I couldn't wait to start a new life across the border as a refugee. So we stowed ourselves on the train, and we made it across the inner German border successfully.

After reaching my destination, I felt like I had stepped into the movies I used to see as a child back in Iran.

Everything I was doing seemed like a scene from a vaguely remembered movie. The reason was that everything felt surreal. It wasn't that it was difficult for me to accept the reality that I was finally in a foreign country. After all, I had traveled to Syria and Turkey only recently. What I found hard to wrap my head around was that I had entered the country illegally. That was the surreal part. It was giving me the chills. I got to admit a part of it was exciting, and I had never done anything so exciting in my life. But I was afraid as well because I was playing on the other side of the law. I was nervous. I felt it was written all over my face that I had entered the country illegally. The people with whom I entered West Germany told me that I should go to the first policeman I see and say, *"Ausländer! Ausländer!"* which means foreigner or refugee in German. Not being able to speak the local language was a huge barrier. It took me a while to learn the word. West Germany was like heaven when compared to other countries where I had gone before. I had never seen a country so advanced and bright. It indeed was an eye-opening experience. I couldn't be on my own for very long in West Germany because I was almost out of money, and I was cold. After walking around for a while, I found a policeman and said the word I was taught to say. I was glad I found a policeman before I could forget the word.

After all, that was the only German word I knew. I repeated the word three or four times in a row. However, what happened next with me was something I wasn't prepared for. The policeman started firing questions at me in the toughest German I could imagine. I couldn't answer a single question. I was escorted by the officer to a police station and appropriately interrogated in the presence of a translator. After being thoroughly questioned, I was sent to a refugee camp. 'Mission accomplished at last,' I thought.

After arriving at the refugee camp, I was shown the room I would share with someone else. The first night I spent there was all about thinking of the people I had left back home. I thought about how no one, not my father, my wife, nor children, had the slightest idea that I had safely made it into West Germany. It was a strange feeling that night. I couldn't believe I had traveled from Esfahan to West Germany. There were several questions in my mind. Was my life going to be better from this point onward? Will I find the purpose of my life here? If you ask me if I felt better in the refugee camp or not, I would say no. That certain sense of loneliness was still with me. The burden of my guilt and shame also never left me. I was still at the mercy of my thoughts and emotions. I may have accomplished my personal goal and joined the refugee camp, but that didn't mean I would be able to see my sons any time soon.

That thought added even further weight to the already existing weight of self-disgust, doubt, and regret. How would I ever be able to face my sons and justify why I had abandoned them in the first place. I consoled myself again by saying that leaving them was the best thing I could ever do for them, as I was not capable of being a good father to them. Had I been with them, my sons would have grown up in my shadow and become like me. I loved my sons too much to let that happen. That's why it was better to this far-off land where nobody knew me and didn't seem to like me.

The year was 1986. After spending a few days in the refugee camp, I came to realize this place was not a very good one. Maybe it was because I was an Iranian. And Iranians sure know how to show hospitality to both fellow Iranians and non-Iranians as well. On the other hand, I found most Germans, if not all, to be opposite. During the time I spent in the refugee camp, I encountered a lot of Germans. I was surprised to see that most of them were rude and did not want refugees in their country. Some never failed to taunt me by saying, *"Ausländer! Ausländer!"* every time they saw me. They would see my dark hair and start using racial slurs. Some bigots they were.

One day I was returning to my room after having lunch when I heard noises outside. I rushed to see what was happening. To my horror, I saw a few German boys beating a refugee in the yard. I heard one of them say, *"There are a lot of refugees in this country, and if a few of them turned up dead, it wouldn't make a big difference."*

That wasn't the only time I witnessed such an incident. There were other incidents where the beating got so intense that the refugee under attack would end up with broken teeth or jaw, and sometimes both.

After witnessing a few beatings, I knew I had to be careful around here. I had to watch every step I take, and every word I speak. Making enemies was the last thing I wanted to do. One night, I went out to a bar for a couple of drinks. I thought a little walk in the fresh air would do me right. I was sitting in the bar, not very far from the camp, having a drink when a German guy came up to me, put his face close to mine and yelled at me, *"What the fuck are you doing in my country?"* When I did not respond, he picked up the almost full mug of beer in front of me and poured it down my head. I was a typical hothead, especially when someone misbehaved with me like that. However, sensing this was not the right moment to pick a fight I just sat down and stared at him without doing anything. I did not retaliate because that could land me in jail. I tolerated the insult.

After the man left, other people in the bar came up to me to tell me that it was very wise of me not rising up to the taunts as the guy had quite a reputation around this area for beating up refugees. They told me that last week he had beaten up a refugee who had ended up with a broken nose and a few broken teeth as well.

I came back from the bar and went to bed. I wouldn't say that the incident did not affect me at all. I could not stand such hatred and violence against innocent people. I may not have the best character, but I was a non-violent and loving person who did anything but pick fight with random people in public places.

Although everyone told me that I had made the smart move and had wisely not replied to the racist guy in the bar, the truth was that I was angry and humiliated by his insults. I had started to become ashamed of my black hair and my identity. I did not want anyone to find out that I was a foreigner. I wanted to be accepted or at least left alone. Instead, what I got was people yelling in my face and telling me they wanted me to get out of their country. I had a feeling of ongoing unrest, and of not belonging anywhere. The only thing that would go around in my head was that my family didn't want me, my country didn't want me, God hated me, and even after coming all the way out here in search of a better life, I was still treated the same way. I was still unwanted. I thought I was useless. I felt I wasn't white enough, I wasn't black enough, and I wasn't good enough.

A person learns from his experiences, and I learned from mine. I became quite careful about what I did, where I went, and what I said in front of Germans. I would be lying if I'd say that all Germans were the same. I lived in Germany for over two and a half years, and during that time, I came across some really caring and understanding Germans as well, who helped me every step of the way. If there weren't any good and kind at heart Germans, why would they be helping refugees in the first place?

Some of the most benevolent and generous people I came to know in Germany belonged to the church community. These people were nice to us and would do all they could do to help us. They would arrange for all of us to get warm clothes and blankets. They would invite us to their homes for dinner, and sometimes to even spend the night if the weather was too cold. It was not all that bad. However, I was just not able to find a comfortable place in between the Germans who were social bigots, and the ones who were kind. I just kept drinking, which got steadily worse as time went by, instead of improving somewhat. I could have let go of the drinking, considering I did not possess any money to buy alcohol because I was a refugee, and I was not allowed to work. However, that did not stop me from getting the one thing I wanted more than anything. That was alcohol. I was fixated on alcohol because it was the only way I knew how to numb my senses and dull my pain. That was my ultimate goal for as long as I was in Germany. I just wanted to get a bottle in my hand that would last me the entire night so that I would escape from who I was.

I think this was the time I had become so used to drinking before going to sleep that I was unable to fall asleep without finishing a bottle. That was the only way I could put my mind at rest. The nights I had to spend without drinking were the toughest. I could not get any sleep for up to three nights. So now I had another reason to drink – to avoid sleep deprivation. Even the guy I shared the room with didn't mind gulping down a glass or two with me at night.

I figured I needed most of my wits if I wanted to survive the refugee camp in West Germany. Sleep deprivation would make me useless for days on end, whereas a hangover was cured almost overnight. So I wanted to take the lesser of the two evils. Those are the type of excuses I gave to myself to allow myself to drink without regret. I got so sick and tired of being called names in public that I had to think about ten times before I went out to do something. I was cursed and picked on in the streets, in the camp, and in the bars to the point that I was ashamed to call myself an Iranian. These incidents just made me wish I was from another country, or that the people of my country were more respected in the world. I had come to Germany thinking that it was among the modern nations of the world and that I would find it easy to start a life here. However, the complete opposite happened. I was unable to start work or go anywhere else for that matter. I definitely couldn't go back to Iran, and I could not go to another country as well. It was like being stuck in limbo. I thought, even if I could go to another country, where would I choose to go? I had no idea where I would go off to. After my experiences in West Germany, I was hesitant to try living in another foreign country. My thoughts were always the same – what if it turns out to be worse than this?

One beautiful evening, I went to the disco and had the opportunity to meet a nice, good looking girl. Although I wasn't looking for company, she seemed smart and funny and was very helpful to me. We spent the evening together and had a great time with each other. We walked the streets and drank coffee. We talked about random things, mostly about her, not me. Where she lived, what she did, what was she passionate about, and what was she studying. I was more interested in knowing about her rather than telling her about me. Spending time with her soothed me. I felt better about myself in her company. When we had called it a night, both of us agreed that we should meet each other again, so we exchanged our numbers. However, she somehow managed to find out that I was a refugee. Maybe she called in, and someone at the facility told her where she was calling. When I called her after waiting a couple of days for her call, she replied, "I thought you were Italian, but now I find out that you are from Iran, and you are a refugee. I cannot see you any more if you are a refugee." Her words broke my heart. I did not want to be a refugee anymore. I could not figure out why the people of Germany were so discriminating against us. She was okay when she thought I was a foreigner from Italy. However, a foreigner from Iran was someone she could not be involved with.

These double standards in the world were beyond me. They made me sick. I thought it was good that we just met once. Had she broken my heart after a couple of dates, I would have fallen in love with her and would have wanted to kill myself probably. For some people, it was effortless to play with other people's emotions. Why they do that and how they find pleasure in doing that, I would never come to understand that.

While I was living in the refugee camp, we were given food boxes every two weeks, containing bread, rice, and other things that we could cook and survive on. All of us used to share our resources, and we managed to get by, even in the winters. In the camp, I met people from all over the world. Almost everyone had a sad story to tell. It hurt me somewhere inside my mostly numb heart, seeing so much devastation and destruction, so much suffering. However, I never shared my story with anyone. I wasn't ready to do that yet. But together, we did something which would make us feel good.

Like I already mentioned, as a refugee, none of us could work in West Germany; hence, we did not have any money of our own. The only way we could get our hands on money was by shoplifting and stealing clothes, booze, and other items and selling them on the street. That was quite an activity for people like us. I was caught twice by the police, luckily they only questioned me and let me go with a few warnings.

There were a few of us in the refugee camp who would get together in the evenings and get drunk together. I can honestly say that I was drunk each and every day of the two and a half years I spent in that camp. I got myself drunk on stolen booze so that I could escape the haunting reality of my life.

At least I tried to!

Chapter 6
Moving to Canada and Continuing My Personal Battle

"I have seen many storms in my life. Most storms have caught me by surprise, so I had to learn very quickly to look further and understand that I am not capable of controlling the weather, to exercise the art of patience and to respect the fury of nature."

– Paulo Coelho

Patience was the only asset I had. And I was afraid I was slowly losing it.

The reason I had come to West Germany was to make my life better. However, my life had taken a turn toward an even darker road in this country. The people here were unfriendly, rude, and almost bordering on being cruel. They had been successful in making me feel ashamed of my identity and nationality. All the refugees here were in the same boat. We did whatever we could to help each other, but we were all so tied up in our misery that it was difficult to stop thinking about it long enough to help anyone else. As I mentioned earlier, we as refugees had resorted to stealing. We would get together in groups and pick a supermarket or a store where we could make a move easily. This so-called modern country had even provided the opportunity for us to turn to a life of crime. I had never stolen things before in my life, but I slowly got the taste of it. All I had to do was walk through a store and act nonchalant. Then when nobody was looking, I had to slip an item or two in my pocket or my bag. After shoplifting items from supermarkets, we would sell them on the streets for money that we used to spend on our own. I used to spend my illegal income on booze.

Sometimes I wonder that West Germany could have easily made sure that we had better lives. However, they were so anti-foreigners that making them a part of society was almost impossible for them. I don't think they were against all foreigners. They didn't like foreigners from the third world and troubled countries.

What I was confused about, more on a human level than a political one, was that if they were not going to accept us and let us become a part of their society, why the hell had they let us seek refuge with them in the first place? Why didn't they ban refugees in their country? This way, the people who sought shelter would have gone to countries that were willing to accept them and lived a more happy and prosperous life.

I was sinking into a bottomless pit of despair because of the behavior of the locals. They had no right to hurt my feelings and make me feel bad about myself. I felt uncomfortable telling people where I came from. Everything related to me had become a taboo subject. So much so, I had stopped asking other refugees questions about their life, and how they had ended up in West Germany. The reason why I stopped interacting with other refugees was that they would have less of a right to ask me the same questions.

That was the time I had increasingly become edgy and short-tempered. It was a direct consequence of drinking excessively. Whenever I reflected on the purpose of my continued existence, I felt at a loss and disturbed. How can a man continue to live with no purpose in life? Whenever I thought about the plans that I had made before coming here, I felt infuriated. I had initially planned to earn good money here and send it back to my children so that they could live a better life, untainted by my disruptive presence. But I wasn't allowed even to earn a dime. Stealing stuff from shops and markets of West Germany was not all that profitable. Moreover, I had no way of sending money without the authorities getting involved and asking a lot of unwanted questions. I wanted to stay under the radar as much as possible.

Considering the tensions between West Germany and East Germany, you never knew when the authorities would identify you as a suspicious person, take you into custody, and deport you. Germans used to throw an attitude at us as if all the refugees should be extremely grateful to them since they had taken us in. I would have been grateful had they paved the way for me to find the kind of life I was looking for. But I got nothing here, nothing but desolateness, hatred, and rejection. I felt so depressed that there were times I used to regret leaving my family and lying to them about where I was going. I used to regret leaving Iran. I wanted to live somewhere that could soothe the turmoil within me. Germany, however, had exacerbated it. My drinking had gotten worse than it was in Istanbul, where frankly, it was entirely wrong. So, I was always finding new lows in my life.

As I said, the refugees mostly kept to themselves, wrapped up in their troubles. So, it was tough for me to strike any meaningful friendship with anyone. However, I did manage to befriend a guy who hung out with me and sometimes drank with me. Most of the time, he was my smoking buddy. We used to smoke cigarettes together and talk about how this place was hell on earth. We used to ponder over the possibilities of finding a way out of there.

Although I did not have a lot of money left and going any place else would require a lot of it, there was no harm in discussing possibilities. There was no way I was going back to Iran. No matter how much I missed my sons, I was not ready to go back there. I wanted to find a better way to live, but I was running out of patience. It seemed the more I searched for a way to find inner peace, the more it eluded me.

This friend I was talking about finally decided he couldn't spend another day in West Germany. He had had enough of this country's refugee treatment, so he decided to leave for Canada in the summer of 1987. Even though I wanted to leave Germany, I did not want to spend a lot of money and end up in another hellhole. So I stayed put, trying to decide my next course of action.

The one smart thing I did was not to lose touch with my friend after he left. We used to write letters and keep each other posted on the latest developments in our lives. We never failed to update each other on our most recent troubles. After a few weeks, my friend wrote a letter in which he couldn't stop praising Canada. He wrote beautiful things about the country he called heaven on earth.

He described to me how people lived there and how easy

it was for everyone to find a place in a society that was determined to lift them. After reading his very first letter, I was sold on the idea of moving to Canada. I wrote back to him, telling him that I wanted to move to Canada as well and that I was ready and willing to take another risk. I also wanted to see the country he so provocatively described as heaven on earth.

In the fall of 1987, I got my friend's reply, saying that he could get me a fake passport if I sent him a couple of my passport-sized photographs. I did as he requested and waited for some good news to come. It was a long time since I had received good news. I was desperate for one. In February 1988, after a couple of months of waiting, the day finally arrived. I got another mail from my friend. Inside the enclosed envelope, there was a passport. I was surprised to see that the name on the passport was Spanish. That means I was supposed to enter Canada as *José Antonio Grazia*.

When I saw the name on the passport, I realized that I needed to change my appearance and mannerism a little bit so that I would appear Spanish. There were a couple of Spanish guys living inside the refugee camp, so I made it a habit to notice them in the following week. I concluded that for my appearance, I would have to grow out my hair a little more. All the Spanish guys I observed seemed to sport long hair.

Other than that, I noticed most Spanish guys had their ears pierced. So I had to get my ear pierced. Never in a million years had I thought I would get my ear pierced. Here I was, sporting an earring in my left ear. I had to imitate being Spanish, so I noticed every particular detail. Spanish guys preferred to wear regular clothing. That was a relief. However, they favored leather jackets over any other kind, so I added that to my get-up as well. There was nothing I could do about speaking Spanish on such short notice. So, I decided to talk only when necessary. That too in German or broken English, keeping my accent as thick as I could. I was concerned about how fake I would look but pushed that thought out of my mind because I was desperate to leave Germany. Had the name on my passport been Japanese, I would have taken the risk of convincing Canadian authorities that I was a Japanese. I wanted to start a new chapter in my life, and I had a feeling that this was the only opportunity I was going to get, and I had to seize it. Carpe diem!

When everything was set, and I was to leave for Canada, I could feel the same rush of excitement inside me that I felt when I was leaving Turkey for West Germany. Considering my hopes got shattered here, I feared how my new life that awaited me in Canada would be like. The plan to get me to Canada involved me first going to Zurich and from there, catching a flight to Canada. My final destination was Toronto. However, I was supposed to land in Montreal from Zurich. I thought of breaking the news to my family that I was moving to Canada for good, but decided I would inform them once I got settled there.

I followed the plan, and from Zurich, I booked a flight to Montreal. I used the fake Spanish passport to board the flight to Montreal. As soon as I landed at the Montreal airport, the first thing I did was I went to the airport bathroom and tore up my fake passport into tiny little pieces and flushed it down the toilet. I then looked for and found a Canadian border official. I walked up to him and declared that I wanted to claim refugee status. I had to go to Toronto, where my friend was. Montreal was just a brief stopover for me. After taking care of all the formalities and paperwork, I was off to Toronto. I took a bus and arrived in Toronto on the morning of the 7th of April, 1988. It took me little time to fall in love with Canada, and in particular, Toronto. The lifestyle of Canadians was something that I found appealing. The thing that I found the most pleasant was that here, there was no discrimination. No one thought that they were superior to someone else. I was not scorned for being an Iranian, nor was I shunned for being a refugee.

People here were welcoming, and they lived in harmony with people from all over the world. Asians, Mexicans, Canadians, Japanese, colored, and white people, people with dark and light hair, everyone was welcome and had found a way to co-exist with each other. People of different origins were able to build and live their lives in peace in Canada. And that's what mattered the most.

The fact that life in Canada was pleasant and that my Iranian nationality would cause no one any problem was clear to me in just a few hours that I spent in the city. I guess that's how long it takes to identify the nature of the people in the city where you are about to start a new life. Nobody in Toronto looked at me the wrong way, and this suddenly boosted my hopes. At the time, I thought that finally, I found a place where I could start building a life for myself. I might be able to let go of my demons and start a decent life with no internal struggles. I believed in the harmony created by the different races living together and thought I might find a place for myself as well. That gave me a sense of belonging that I had not felt in a long time. Even though I was in a new place, I was not feeling suffocated as I did in West Germany.

The best thing about Canada was that refugees were

allowed to work and earn money. They were able to make a life for themselves away from their homes, unlike West Germany, where refugees were utterly dependent on the government for their upkeep. Due to this reason, after receiving my work visa, I did not waste any time in finding a job. I couldn't wait to carve my niche in what seemed to be the land of opportunities. My first job in Canada was with a company that manufactured aluminum windows.

The work wasn't bad, and I was thankful that I was finally earning some money. That was the money that I had made through honest, hard work, and not through stealing. My friend helped me further and let me move into his three-bedroom apartment, which he shared with two other guys. I was more than comfortable and happy with my new life. I didn't remember the last time I was so pleased and content with my life. I had a roof over my head, and I was earning my keep. That was all I wanted. Even though I was still drinking, I was happy how my life had turned out to be. What a relief it was! Finally, I was on the road to becoming somebody. Good days never last forever. Whoever said that was a genius. Just as I had settled down and started appreciating my life for a change, life threw a curveball my way once again. Bad things always happen without warning. And the same thing happened to me. While I was on the job,

I ended up injuring my shoulder. It was a severe injury, one that didn't allow me to do manual work that I had been doing.

However, I received a lump sum settlement of $26,000 as a worker's compensation. It was a reasonable settlement. The amount would last me for quite some time, provided that I spent it wisely. Since I did not have a job anymore, I decided to enroll in a school to improve my English language. The program I opted for was in the daytime, and I was even able to obtain student aid to cover some of the expenses. For once, I was considering making my situation better and not just wasting my time away with drinking.

Even after the injury, I was happy with the way things had turned out. I wasn't in the ideal situation, but I was able to stabilize my situation without letting it get worse. The only thing that was not under my control was my drinking. On top of that, I had started smoking weed as well. I had considered quitting both habits but hadn't started working on it. Every time I thought about quitting, I would start smoking and drinking even more.

Besides drinking and smoking weed, there were other things I was fond of in my life. For the first time in my life, I was courting a girl. Her name was Chantelle, and she was a French-Canadian brunette with striking charm and poise. The thing that drew me closer to her was that she took an interest in me from the first day we met. Soon, spending time with Chantelle became the best part of my day. I used to look forward to the moments that I would spend with her all day long. She filled the empty void in my life and replaced the loneliness I suffered from in a significant way. We used to spend days and evenings together, and she used to help me with my English.

Chantelle had an excellent job with a telephone company, but she never looked down upon me. She had a caring and loving nature. Once, she took me to Quebec and introduced me to her parents. Although she did have feelings for me, Chantelle dumped me after two years. It wasn't easy for her, but she had to make a decision. She took this drastic step because of me. Had it been any other girl instead of Chantelle, she would have done the same. She was tired of my smoking and drinking, as well as my low self-esteem and constant self-doubt. No matter how much she tried to bolster my self-esteem and self-confidence, I would always end up back where I started from, and then the drinking and smoking would get worse.

With that, the era of the 80s came to an end, and a new decade of my life started.

The year 1990 found me living in a nicely furnished bachelor apartment in the Don Mills and Eglinton Area. The condo was comfortably furnished, and I was quite delighted that I was finally living the way I always wanted to. The money that I had received as a worker's compensation helped me decently furnish the apartment. However, the one thing I failed to check before moving to this area was the neighborhood. I was not aware of the fact that the neighborhood was a little shady. There were all sorts of illicit activities going on around that area, like drug dealing and prostitution. I only found out about it after I had settled down into my new home. Before that, nothing unusual or suspicious came to my notice.

The neighborhood had seemed quite reasonable to my untrained eyes. I say untrained because I was new to Canada and did not know what to look for. During the first two years, everything about Canada seemed merely incredible. The way the Canadians lived seemed like they were living in luxury. For me, it was a luxury because I was used to living in much harsher living conditions. Even in the refugee camp, everything was dingy and dark than it was in this bright and posh country. Even the seedy neighborhoods here seemed good to me. I minded my own business and continued to live in that apartment until I met Joanne. She was from England.

After we went out together a couple of times, Joanne told me she was engaged to someone else. I was bowled over. I didn't know how to react. The only question that popped into my mind was, what exactly was she doing with me then? When I asked her, she told me it was nothing to worry about. It turned out she and her fiancé had an arrangement. They could see other people outside their relationship if they wanted to. They were not restricted to companionship by their engagement. Joanne called this unusual arrangement an understanding. But there was something else about Joanne that I didn't know. After we had been going out for a few weeks, I realized Joanne was bisexual. She was attracted to girls just as much she took an interest in guys. That was a whole new territory for me. For a time, I was not sure how I should react to it, but then I did what I usually did, took the whole notion of being bisexual in my stride. I mean, I ignored the fact as much as possible.

My relationship with Joanne turned out to be an unhealthy and fatal one. Not because she was bisexual, but because she was into heavy drinking and smoking. When I had a company like Joanne, what do you expect I did? I ended up getting drunk. No matter how hard I tried to quit, I could not give up these two of my filthy habits. It was like I had developed a bond with alcohol and weed over the years that

I could not break easily. I did not stop even when excessive smoking and drinking began to take a toll on my psychological state. Whenever I messed up a plan or failed to keep a promise, I had a ready-made excuse, *"It was not me. It was the booze."* To which Joanne would scoff and roll her eyes and turn her head away, not talking to me for a while. That made me drink and smoke even more because I wanted to forget all the mistakes I was making under the heavy influence of alcohol and weed.

One night when I was drunk, one of my neighbors, a woman named Lisa, knocked on my door and asked me if she could borrow some money. She explained that she wanted to buy something fundamental from around the corner. Even though I did not have a problem lending her money, my curiosity got the best of me, and I asked her what she was going to buy at this hour. At first, she wouldn't tell me, but when I insisted, she relented and finally told me that she was going to buy some cocaine. I loaned her some money and let her go.

But when Lisa came back, I found myself sitting with her and asking her to let me try cocaine at least once. She looked at me with lifeless eyes and told me not to go down this path. However, I was justifying it in my head that I would do it only once, and that would be the end of it; no more cocaine for me after that. At first, Lisa did not agree. But I was persistent that she let me try it once, so she had to. I reminded her that I was the one who had paid for it, so, technically, it was my stuff she was smoking. In the end, we both ended up smoking crack, allowing its effect to transport us to a world that seemed like a parallel universe without any tension, stress, or worry.

Cocaine is such an addiction. I have no words to describe it. Smoking it once was enough to discover the pleasures of it. The feeling, the sensation that I felt when I dragged, was like I took a straight flight to heaven. I felt weightless. I felt as if I was levitating in the air. That's how I would describe my first experience with crack. I wished I had discovered this magical white powder sooner. Things would have been so much easier for me. I thought alcohol made me forget my issues and get away from my problems, but I was wrong. Crack did the same thing, only so much better and faster than alcohol ever could. Smoking made me feel I was at a different place where none of the tragedies of my life could take hold of me. Crack transported me to the land of no worries. And the best part was that it intensified the feelings of contentment and serenity. It became my true love in an instant, no second thoughts about that.

I never knew that smoking crack that night was my first

step toward hell. It was like I discovered a bottomless pit in which I could fall endlessly. From that point onward, my life began to slip through my hands. It was like I had no control over my life. My life started going downhill once I graduated to crack from alcohol. I was drinking and smoking crack, and I was doing all this while I was unemployed. That meant that I was running out of my $26,000 fast. I was losing everything that I had. I was destroying my life, and I was unable to stop myself even if I wanted to.

The truth was that I didn't want to live anymore. I just wanted to die and finally get some peace from all the shame and guilt swirling around inside me. I had failed at everything I tried to do, and this was it. I could not go on trying anymore. I wanted to die, as simple as that. Back then, I believed no force in this world could stop me from ending my life. It was better for me to stay tangled in the web of crack and alcohol. I had found solace in addiction. That's what I believed in. I didn't know what was wrong with me.

There were nights when I used to wander in the streets, trying to figure out what to do. Sometimes I would forget the way back to my apartment. I was so high that I failed to recognize the same streets and roads that I walked every day. In the morning, I had no idea where I was last night, and who brought me back to my apartment. Did I come back home myself, or did someone bring me back to my apartment? I used to ask myself that question because I had no clear memory of last night. Sometimes, the situation was worse than that. Sometimes I failed to get back home and used to wake up the next morning on a park bench. And I had no idea how I got there. I continued to spend my days and nights like that, so what happened next was bound to happen. One night, I was driving back home under the influence of crack and alcohol, and I drove into the car in front of mine. As a result, I wrecked my car. Of course, I didn't even have insurance at the time. It was a terrible blow. It was a dreadful episode.

In the middle of one night, I woke up feeling confused. As I sat on my bed, trying to recollect the events of the last few hours, I noticed that the wooden flooring in my room was burning. The walls seemed smoked. And the curtains were already burned to a crisp. I realized that my apartment was on fire. I had fallen asleep with a lit cigarette in my hand. As a result, a large section of my house was destroyed that night. However, I managed to get out of there before the flames engulfed my bed. After I caught hold of reality, I thought, how on earth was I not roasted like a steak? Had the cigarette fallen on my bed instead of the floor, I would have been the first one to catch fire.

A part of me wished it would have been that way. At least, I wouldn't have to live through another day, smoking crack and drinking alcohol. I was so stoned I didn't wake up from the smoke in the room or from the heat of the flames. It was when the fire had started getting out of control that I woke up. After the incident at my apartment, I forced myself to find a job. I found one at a Greek restaurant. I started as a dishwasher, but the owner of that restaurant suggested I attend a bartending school so that I could manage the restaurant bar. It seemed like a good idea to me. Thus, I started attending bartending classes. Soon I got the job of the bartender that the owner promised me. During those days, when I was tending the bar, I had cut back on my drinking, and I was doing considerably well. I even managed to stay sober for a few days. But life never got tired of throwing curveballs my way. It wasn't long before I realized that the employees locked the doors of the restaurant after hours and had a private party. They helped themselves to the restaurant's liquor and got drunk for free.

All the staff, including the waitresses, used to party almost every night. I enjoyed the free alcohol and started stealing some from the bar too. However, like most things in my life, this phase also did not last. The owner found out that I had started drinking too much alcohol from the bar, and it showed from my behavior, which was not suitable for the customers. My performance was getting affected, so the owner fired me.

That was the end of my time as a bartender. I did not want to work that job anyway. I just wanted to smoke crack and drink alcohol and forget everything. That night on my way home, I stopped to ask a prostitute where I could buy some crack. She led me to a dark alley where two guys suddenly showed up. They beat me up and stole all of my money. That was when I started thinking about committing suicide. I think that was the first time that wicked thought crossed my mind. However, something stopped me from taking any drastic measures to end my life. Maybe the idea of smoking crack kept me alive. I knew crack was enough to dull my pain for the time being. So I started living a destructive lifestyle once again.

Chapter 7
A New Destination – Vancouver

"Addiction isn't about substance - you aren't addicted to the substance, you are addicted to the alteration of mood that the substance brings." –**Susan Cheever**

What was I doing with myself? Where was my life heading? Just when I thought I had my life under control, I was on the brink of losing it again. Soon after I had lost the job at the Greek restaurant, I had started to derail once again. Every bad habit that I had, namely drinking and crack, had multiplied tenfold, and I had no idea what I was supposed to do. I was utterly clueless. I don't know if the desire to put my life on the right track ever left me. But why was I not able to drive a change in my life? Why was my willpower so low?

Why did I ever come to Canada in the first place? I used to ask myself. The very intention was to improve my life so that I could support myself and my family. So that somehow I could just put the pieces of my life together. I did want to make my life better so that I could have a good relationship with my boys. Then why did I keep on making more of a mess, out of my life? There was nothing I could do to improve my life now. That is what I used to think all the time. My head was exploding with negative thoughts, and I blamed my childhood experiences for it; the way my father had lied to me about my mother, how my step-brother had treated me, how I was molested, and how I was continuously beaten by my brother-in-law. I also thought of my experiences in the war, in Syria, and in West Germany, where I became a victim of severe racism that continues to haunt me. I was caught in the web of never-ending self-pity, guilt, shame, and hatred for myself. I couldn't stop blaming every disturbing event I went through in my life and every person who was unfair to me. I had no power to prevent the way I was thinking.

I was falling into a pit of depression, and I didn't even know that. There were days when I thought this is the day I end my life. For me, that was the best solution to all my problems. It would stop all the hassles of my life once and for all. But at the same time, I thought it was pathetic that I was even entertaining these thoughts. I had always believed that life was something that was meant to be lived to the fullest. There was supposed to be meaning behind it. I think that is the reason that I had tried and finally succeeded in escaping from Iran. In that country, people just blindly followed what they were told to do, and everyone kept telling me what to do and how to live my life. I couldn't do that any longer. Other people telling me what to do with my life was something that always bothered me. How could they know what was best for me? They were not the ones who had to live inside my skin and my head. They just came into my life and made important decisions for me and then walked right out, leaving me to deal with the consequences. My parents had decided that it was time for me to get married, and someone else decided who my partner was going to be. And just like that, I was forced into marriage. It was like everyone was ready to play with my mind and my life. These thoughts that came into my mind resulted in making me angry and depressed. As I have said, this combination of anger, guilt, and depression made my substance abuse even worse. As a result, I got beaten by two thugs. I got beaten up pretty bad.

That sudden incident shook the earth beneath my feet. I had thought that the girls who worked the streets were heavy users. So, I approached a working girl and asked her where I could buy some crack. After throwing a glance at me she asked me to follow her, and I was attacked in a stinking alley from behind. I was punched in the face. I was kicked in the stomach. I was robbed. For days, I had difficulty in breathing. When I used to draw breath, I used to feel a sharp throbbing of pain in my lungs.

How, by any stretch of your imagination, can you say that I deserved what happened with me? Why did that happen with me the same night I lost my job? How was it fair? Life was taking way too much from me, and it wasn't giving me back anything in return. I hoped that death would come to me and end my suffering. I was no good to anyone this way. I was worse than useless. If my sons ever saw me like this, they would be ashamed to have me as their father.

I was so desperate to take on any given opportunity to end my life that when some of my friends asked me to go to Vancouver with them, I couldn't say yes right away. It took a lot of convincing for me to say yes finally. It turned out, saying yes on an impulse was one of the better decisions I had made lately at that time. It was just as good as deciding to come to Canada. My friends told me that Vancouver was a beautiful city. There was nothing better than visiting the town in the spring season. And they were right.

I packed everything I owned, which was not much at this point, and left for Vancouver. I had nothing to lose in Toronto. I was jobless and had no one to answer to. So I could take a chance and try my luck in Vancouver as well.

Deep down, I was thinking that moving to a new city would help me escape my demons. I had tried to lower my substance abuse after that night in the alley. So, after a long time, I was thinking of positive thoughts, and it looked to me that my life would finally get back on track.

We traveled to Vancouver in a silver Mazda 626, which was an excellent car. That road trip was a pleasant experience. That was when I truly realized how beautiful Canada was. It was a scenic drive, and even though I was used to seeing beautiful mountains in Iran, I was blown away by the snowcapped mountains that we passed on our way to Vancouver. It was a long journey. And by long, I mean long. It took us ten days to reach Vancouver. On the way, we used to stop at hotels, stay the night, take some sleep, and continue traveling in the morning. I particularly loved it when we drove at night with a star-studded sky above us. I remember every detail of that experience.

This journey did me some good. I felt there were good things in this world to live for. But I didn't know how exactly I was supposed to do that. I would obsess over how I wanted to change my life, but it kept turning back to drugs, booze, and failure. I was looking for something. I knew that much at least. That is why I continued moving. Although what I was looking for escaped my mind altogether. Maybe I was trying to find a way to escape from my addictions, or perhaps I thought there was a better life waiting for me someplace other than where I currently was. I had no clear idea of what would happen when I reach Vancouver. I was hoping it would be a pleasant experience for me, but what happened was entirely the opposite.

After having an incredible journey, the three of us finally arrived. Immediately upon arrival, we were faced with the question of lodging. Where were we going to stay? Fortunately for me, I had stayed in contact with a female friend who had stayed with me and worked at the Greek restaurant where I used to bartend not long ago. So for about a week, I stayed with her. After that, I started looking for an apartment to rent with my friends. Much to our delight, we found an apartment within a week in the Metrotown Area. It was a good find, and we moved in right away.

After we had moved in, we started a routine that complemented one another. In the mornings, we went to work, and then in the evenings, we would all go out for exploratory walks. We used to walk around the blocks near our apartment. We wanted to find out what was there in our neighborhood. We wanted to find out what options we had to pass the time in the evenings. It was during one of these walks that the three of us noticed a casino in a shopping mall.

Up until that moment, I had never seen a casino, let alone be inside one. It was a little tempting for me to see something that I had heard so much about but had never actually seen. My only experience with gambling had been playing blackjack as a kid, back in Iran.

I couldn't believe I was standing in front of a real live casino. Soon I was able to convince my friends that we should try our luck in a casino. My friends did not need much persuading. We were bored with spending lonely and dull evenings and were desperate for a change. And the casino seemed like a beautiful place to have some fun and party the night away after so long. Without giving the chance of entertaining ourselves in a casino another thought, we went in. The first thing that hit me when we walked into the casino was the soundscape of the place. The music playing over there was loud, and it seemed people were laughing in every corner of the casino. The entire soundscape of the area was punctuated with the dinging of the slot machines. The next thing that hit me was the smell. I could smell booze and cigarette in the air. The interior of the place was a treat for the eyes: bright lights, fancy décor, and vibrant faces served my eyes a feast to remember. It took me and my friends at least half an hour to adjust to the atmosphere. After we had caught hold of our senses, which seemed to have run haywire after coming in, we were introduced to our first table game. Of course, I lost money in that game. But guess what? I had fun.

When I think of my experience in that casino, I feel I have a thing for bad habits; habits that have the potential to destroy you! I just seemed to have no trouble at all in adopting any of those habits; be it smoking crack, drinking, and now gambling. I wasn't sure if I was ready to afford another dangerous addiction. I sure have that sort of personality that readily adopts addictive behaviors.

Just like it had been with crack, I was hooked on the game in no time at all. It was something new to distract me, and I was all for it. I did not realize it at the time that I was displaying the sort of behavior that was indicative of mental health problems. I was doing things that were not good for me. I was destructive. I kept thinking that I could control my drinking and my drug problems, but they were way past my control. My substance abuse was, however, not just a way for me to escape my reality; it was a part of a broader issue. I wasn't aware of how much it had affected my life, and how much this behavior had become part of my personality.

However, there is one thing I know. If it hadn't been for my substance abuse problem, I would have committed suicide a long time ago. Just as these addictions provided a way for me to escape my reality, it was these drugs that distracted me from the thoughts about taking my own life.

It seemed the only thing I was good at in my life was addictions. I hated it when someone else controlled my life, yet I happily allowed my cravings to take control of my life. I became addicted to gambling. The little money that I earned, I used to spend that on gambling. Of course, I wasn't lucky enough to win big, but I had fun wasting money. It took my mind off things. The same pattern of my life continued until my father came to visit me in 1994. I was in contact with my family, and they showed interest in visiting me, but I only allowed my father to come. I wasn't emotionally fit enough to face any other member of my family. I was shocked to see my father. He looked old and feeble. I wasn't earning much at the time. Still, I was able to pay for his ticket.

I had a strange relationship with my father. I did, of course, love him as he was my father, and I had seen him work hard to provide for us, but there was always this grudge I had against him. I had never forgiven him for what he did with my mother and me when I was only a 6-month-old infant. He separated me from my mother and never told me that the woman I thought was my mother, was not my birth mother. It was, for this reason, I always felt uncomfortable in his presence.

The time I chose to invite my father was a good time for me. I had my apartment and a decent income. I even had my car, and I was going to school as well. I wanted my father to see that I had done well for myself. I wanted him to be proud of me. My father had an old habit of smoking opium. Back in Iran, opium was a part of our tradition. There, it was given like a gift, like chocolates or flowers.

It was not something that people did in hiding. However, in Canada, smoking opium was frowned upon. My father couldn't live without smoking opium every night, so he continued to smoke in Canada as well. I had to explain to him that it was not considered polite in Canada to smoke opium in public. So he smoked inside the apartment. The way he craved for opium made me see my reflection in him. He was an addict too, but I did not tell him about my use of crack.

While my father was living with me, I was seeing a Caucasian girl named Christine. This girl loved me and was ready to accept me with my addictions. She managed to put up with my drinking and drugs. She tried to make me stop smoking crack and drinking alcohol, but I never paid that much attention to her. I never listened to her. I was just too wrapped up in my world to care about how she was feeling. Looking back now, I do not like the way I treated her. She was trying to help me. She put up with my drunken rages and bouts of depression.

She did her best to try and cheer me up and make me see the positive side of life and myself. However, it was all to no avail. Even though I mistreated her, and she did not like me smoking crack, she always allowed me to come over and smoke it while my father was living with me. All of this added to my guilt because I knew I was not treating her right. I was selfish, inconsiderate, and I was dishonest and disloyal to her. She loved me and tried to make my life better, but shoved her aside and cheated on her. That is something that I regret to this day.

The other girl that I was seeing was Iranian. I want to call her Becky in this book. She was a sweet girl who took good care of me. I had never told her anything about my drug use and a drinking problem. She never knew anything about it back then. However, a mutual friend of ours who lived in the same building told Becky about my relationship with Christine. Becky was furious, and she did everything she could to make my life miserable after that. When I broke up with her, I went through some legal problems that she created. Becky knew I was getting my citizenship in 1994, so she tried to give me some tough time. Since I had no criminal record, I was able to get out of the mess she had created for me. However, these legal problems caused even more chaos in my life. That was the pattern of my life. I would try to get better, but then something would happen that would shatter the delicate balance that I had managed to find, and then I would derail again.

After the chaos that Becky caused in my life, I felt my life turning upside down once again. As a result, I started abusing drugs and alcohol even more. Every effort that Christine had put into controlling my habits went to waste within a week. After that, my life started taking another turn for the worse. My finances went downhill, and I began to get irritated with my life. I was irritated with my father and was not in a good mental state around him. Even though his visa was for six months, I wanted him to go back to Iran, after just a couple of months. I felt as if he was becoming a burden on me, a nuisance that I couldn't put up with anymore. I had to pretend to be someone I was not while he was there. He knew next to nothing about my substance abuse, so I could not even smoke or drink in my own home, which was a major problem for me.

After I started drinking heavily again, I just wanted to be

alone. Knowing that my father would be at home, I used to spend hours and hours drinking at Christine's apartment. I first went to her house, listen to a long lecture from her, during which we would end up in a fight, and then I would find myself in an even worse mood. The rest of the night, I spent it drinking and smoking, which in turn made the whole experience pathetic. My life had become tedious again, and I wanted my father out of my life as soon as possible. So somehow, I managed to convince my father that it would be for the best if he went back to Iran.

Even though he was determined to stay for the whole six months, I was able to change his mind. I said soon the winter season would arrive, and it would be bad for his health. I took him on a few sightseeing trips, one of which was to Victoria, and sent him off back to Iran. I felt terrible that I was sending my father back before his visa expired, but I was helpless. I had no other option. In the last few weeks, I spent with my father. I was not in a good state of mind. I could barely force a smile on my face during the trip we took together. However, I never misbehaved with him or said something rude to him that would show that I was fed up with his presence in my home. At least, I tried not to give away my true feelings. But I guess he was my father. He must have guessed I was trying to get rid of him.

I was so ashamed by my behavior that I brought my father a lot of gifts to make up for my rude behavior. The whole time my father was with me, the shame and guilt of leaving my sons kept eating me like a moth eats cloth. To make it up to my kids, I brought some gifts for them as well and gave them to my father to pass them along to my sons.

After my father left, and I had the entire apartment to myself, I was finally free to do whatever I liked to do at home. Soon I realized that I was, in fact, not a good boyfriend for Christine. She didn't know I had been cheating on her the whole time I was dating her. Also, she was way too good for me. One day, I found out that Christine was seeing someone else, which she had every right to do. I wasn't capable of being a good boyfriend. I wasn't capable of caring for someone. I wasn't capable of having an intimate relationship with anyone. I could not care about other people's feelings. Whenever I was in a relationship, I couldn't be myself. I had to get drunk or high because otherwise, I would not have the confidence or self-esteem to approach anybody.

Soon after Christine found a new boyfriend, we parted our ways. I was happy for her. But at the same time, I felt sad and lonely. She had been my companion and a loyal friend, and I missed having her in my life. I had a charming apartment with beautiful furniture on the 16th floor near English Bay at Davie Street and Jervis, but I had no one to share it with. My loneliness made me destructive. It was killing me. I had a few friends with whom I used to drink and smoke and party, but they weren't always there for me. They had lives of their own. I was sick of my loneliness and was living a dysfunctional life. After Christine and I broke up, I got back to being an alcoholic and crack addict without any further delay. It was almost as if I broke up with Christine to become a junkie. As a result of my reckless lifestyle, I ended up losing my apartment.

I had chased my dream to Canada, the idea of being a good person with a good life. However, I felt I was light years away from fulfilling that dream. Back then, I had no clear understanding of the mental problems I was suffering from. I didn't understand that all the addictions I was dealing with were my response to an illness that needed treatment. I didn't know that addiction is an illness. I didn't believe I was ill. I didn't realize I needed help. I didn't know that all the pain, and trauma, and family problems that I had been through had affected me and were holding me back from living my life to its fullest. All I knew was that I didn't come to Canada to be the person I was and to live the life I was living. That thought led me to feel ashamed of who I was.

Some of my friends knew about my condition, and some didn't. Those who knew tried to help me in whatever way they could. Of course, all their attempts to make me quit crack and booze had proved to be futile. Since I lost my apartment, one of my friends that came with me from Toronto said we should get a lovely, two-bedroom apartment. So we rented one on Beach Avenue on the 23rd floor, overlooking the ocean. I wasn't a useful member of society. I was ashamed of the fact that I wasn't a productive member of the community, and I wasn't a proud Canadian either. For most of my life, I had to live with that guilt.

I liked the new apartment I had moved into. It was a beautiful place, and I had earned a decent amount of money as well. Still, on the weekends, which I spent getting wasted, I would end up in a cheap hotel on Main & Hastings with a crack pipe and a prostitute. Those weekends had become an essential part of my routine. I would be lying if I say I didn't look forward to those weekends. I had no clue why I was doing that. I had no idea why I went to that awful hotel in the first place. It wasn't like I stayed sober the entire week and used drugs only on the weekends. On weekdays, I used to do the same at home. One night, I was in my apartment with my friend, Yassa, smoking crack and drinking, when there was a sudden knock on the door. We tried to hide the booze and crack, but there wasn't enough time. I could feel my knees go weak when I answered the door. There were two police officers at my door with a warrant for my arrest. Becky had lent me some money, and I had paid her back at different times, but I didn't ask her for a receipt. Taking advantage of the situation, she went to a small claims court, and I was sent a notice. However, I didn't respond to the notice because I honestly didn't care about it. I was anxious about the police finding out we were using crack. However, the police saw all of the drug paraphernalia on the table and never charged me over that. As for the notice, I went back to court and took care of the matter in a few days.

In 1997, my addiction had become so bad that I could barely pay my share of the apartment's rent. So I moved out of the lovely apartment I had co-rented with my friend and moved to a small apartment in the West End. Sadly, by the end of every month, I wasn't left with enough money to pay the rent of this apartment as well. Consequently, I lost my home, and I had no place to go. I would sometimes walk in the streets for nine or ten hours before I could find a place to sleep.

A friend of mine from Toronto named Frank was living

with Yassa. I thought maybe they could help me, so I went to visit them. I was tired and exhausted, and I just wanted to sleep. Frank and Yassa were well-aware of my condition. When I asked them if I could spend the night at their place, they told me they had to go somewhere really important. I got the feeling that they just wanted me to leave, so I left. I didn't want to be a burden over somebody. I had no place to sleep, and I just wanted to crash somewhere. So I went to a restaurant on Denman called the Falafel King and met a guy named Jerry. I told him I was homeless with no place to sleep and no money. I told him I would be applying for welfare soon.

Jerry was friendly and kind to me. He said, "No problem," and allowed me to stay in his one-bedroom apartment near Nicola Street for the next eight months. I will never forget the generosity of this man.

While I was living at Jerry's place, I started working for a company that did furniture cleaning and carpet cleaning for Eaton's departmental store. Although I had lost my home and spent sleepless nights in the streets, like beggars, I still hadn't learned my lesson. As soon as I used to find a place to stay and started to earn some money, I started drinking again. After spending eight months at Jerry's home, I moved out of that place and got my apartment at Cardero & Haro Street.

It became a routine for me. After every few months, I would start a new life all over again with a new job and a new place to live. Then a few months would pass, and I would be back in the street, homeless and penniless. The highlight of the new life that I started was a girl that I met at a club. She was pretty and took an interest in me. The next thing I knew, I was dating her. This girl I was slowly falling for was from a well-known family in West Vancouver's British Properties. She, too, wanted to take care of me and get me some professional help. When I had to meet her, I used to stay sober. The minute she would walk out of my apartment, I would start using crack. This girl told me she would do anything for me. She was so caring that she let me use her ATM debit card whenever I asked her to loan me some extra cash. One night she left her ATM debit card at my place, and that same night I went to ATM ten times and withdrew $40 each time. I just had to smoke crack, or else I felt my head would burst. I had to silence the noise in my head, and the only way to do that was to smoke crack. The next day when my girlfriend came, she was angry and tried to talk some sense into me. She told me about her friend, whose boyfriend used to be an alcoholic. But ever since he joined a treatment center, he was no longer drinking. When she told me that, I said, *"Poor guy."* I meant that I felt terrible for the guy because he couldn't drink. I was so indifferent toward life that I mocked this guy's recovery. In contrast, I, myself, was dying and had no clue what was going on.

This girl went out of her way to help me out. She gave me a cat for my birthday and said, *"Maybe you need some love."* One night I was hammered, and I was smoking crack when I noticed the cat staring at me silently from a corner of my living room. The cat knew that I was suffering, and it was looking in my eyes, feeling sorry for me. That moment was devastating. I will never be able to put that moment in the back of my mind.

My girlfriend told me I needed to get help. She said, "Do whatever you must do. I can't go on seeing you like this anymore."

That was when I realized my addiction to crack and alcohol was part of a much bigger problem. That was when I felt like I really should get professional help. I had severe issues that needed treatment. I called the SPCA, and they came and took the cat. The next call I made was to the emergency helpline operator. I said, *"I have a problem with drugs, and I've been drinking a lot lately. I need help."* The operator said, *"No problem. I will give you the detox number."* I honestly had no idea what a detox was. It felt as if it was some hospital. In Iran, my mother used to put opium in my milk when I wouldn't stop crying. The opium used to calm me down. So I thought they would take me to a hospital and carry out blood transfusion because drugs were mixed in my blood since my childhood. I asked the operator what a detox was, and she said, *"It's a facility to help you out. You will find out more details when you go there."* A minute after that, I found myself sitting on my bed with the detox number in my hand. I just had to take the first step toward recovery by dialing that number.

Chapter 8
The Road to Healing

"Healing takes courage, and we all have courage, even if we have to dig a little to find it." –***Tori Amos***

It turned out I wasn't going to have a blood transfusion at the detox. The staff at Cordova Detox did a detailed checkup of mine and kept me under observation for a week before referring me to what was my first treatment center. I went to get my first treatment in 1998. I never thought I had any mental health issue, so I thought maybe they'll suggest some invasive procedure, and I'll be okay after that.

I was very determined to take the treatment center seriously. I attended the meetings and went through the entire recommended procedure for the next three months. I went to the gym and ate healthy, as I was instructed. I was so sure I was healed that I told a guy there, I will never drink or use drugs again. I used to say it so boldly that I could have passed all the lie detector tests. But guess what happened. I left the treatment center, and after two days, I was loaded again.

I was shocked by my behavior. I used to say what's going on with me, am I crazy? Why did I do that? I spent three months in my first treatment center and ended up doing drugs again. I thought I was the weakest person on the face of the earth. I had no self-control and no willpower. I despised myself for getting back to where I started from. I kept on drinking and using crack for the following seven months. It was then I thought of giving myself another chance. Thus, I signed up for another detox plan and spent a week there. This detox center sent me to the second treatment center called "*Kinghaven*" in Abbotsford. I stayed there for 45 days. Even though I only attended the meetings and did not follow the program, I felt a remarkable change in myself.

Staying sober for an entire day felt refreshing, and I realized I had the energy to do productive things in the world. I stayed sober for the next five and a half years. Yes, that was a huge step forward for me. During these five and a half years, a lot of significant events took place in my life.

The first positive thing I did in my sobriety was to start my own business. It was a furnace heating and carpet cleaning business. I felt excited to start a business of my own. After all, that was something I always wanted for myself. I did well in that business. A day came when I had 18 to 20 employees working for me, and I had 5 to 6 trucks. The best thing was that I was sending money back home to

Iran for my kids. I honestly felt proud of myself. I was slowly evolving into a person I dreamed of becoming. Life didn't feel as bad as it used to. I realized there are good things in the world to live for. I started to feel my life was meaningful and that I was a good person, by taking care of my children by sending some money back home every month. After a few months of recovery, I started missing my family so much that nothing interested me more than visiting Iran and seeing my mother, sister, and sons. The big question in my mind was, can I even go to Iran? Considering that I ran away from the country, trying to avoid investigation, I had doubts. What if they arrest me upon my arrival? At that point, I wasn't ready to start a new tragic phase in my life.

So what I did was ask my family to find out if it was safe for me to come to Iran for a few days. My family discussed my case with the authorities and informed me that I was allowed to visit Iran. There were some changes in the policies made by the government over the years, and it was safe for me to return. So I packed up my things and visited Iran for the first time since I left several years ago. I knew my visit would be a nostalgic one and would bring back a lot of memories. However, I never knew it would disrupt my life again.

The plan was to go to Iran and spend two months with my

family. I was looking forward to it eagerly. I couldn't imagine what it would feel like to see my sons and hold them in my arms after such a long time. I was nervous and emotional. I couldn't wait to see my mother and her family. I wondered how she had become after all these years. I was sober for five and a half years now, and that gave me the confidence to face my family, especially my sons. I guess my sobriety was what gave me the courage to plan the visit to Iran in the first place. When my father picked me up from the airport, and I reached home, my sons were already there to greet me. Just one look at them, and I couldn't hold my tears back. Water filled my eyes, and I cried. Nobody could imagine how much I had missed my sons all those years. I just wished I could say that to them. They were grown up. They looked so different. The first few words that fell out of my mouth when I hugged them were, *"I'm so sorry."* I kept saying that for as long as I held them in my arms.

This reaction was expected of me. So, I can't say I made a scene in front of my sons. I had to apologize to them for abandoning them in the age when they needed their father the most. I asked them if they remembered me. My elder son said yes, and the younger one said he had a figure of mine in his head, like a shadow, but he didn't remember my face. He had only seen me in pictures. His reply made me hug him even tighter. I kept kissing his forehead and let my emotions run through my eyes.

My reaction was similar when I held my stepmother, Nosrat, in my arms and my sister, Zahra. Everyone looked so grown up different. There was so much to talk about. There was so much to listen to. I had missed so much in all these years. I wanted to catch up on everything that had happened in Esfahan while I was not there. And of course, I had to visit Shiraz to meet my mother as well. After spending a few weeks in Esfahan with my family, I took my sons to Shiraz. That, too, was an emotional experience for me. All the way, I told my sons about my childhood. Of course, I shared only the good memories, which were only a few. There was so much to talk to with my sons. I was interested in everything about them. What color they liked the most, what sport they were interested in, what festival they enjoyed the most, and what food they liked the most. The more I talked to them and learned about them, the more I realized how important it is for a father to see his sons grow up. It was so unfortunate that I missed all those beautiful years. That day, it hurt me to ask my sons all these basic questions like a stranger trying to get to know another stranger.

I tried to interact with my sons as much as possible. I told them what I used to do when I was their age. What I liked doing and what I disliked. I told them what I was doing in Canada, and how the country looked like. I got them excited about Vancouver and made them want to visit Canada. When my younger son asked me if he could come to Vancouver and live with me, I instantly said yes. I said that would make me very happy. The one thing my sons never asked me was why I left in a hurry and never came back. I guess Mehry must have told them. I didn't want to ask them what they knew about my past because I was trying to avoid the questions that would follow. I was afraid I might not have suitable answers that they would understand.

However, I asked them to apologize to Mehry for me. My visit to Shiraz was just incredible. Seeing my uncles and their grownup kids brought back a lot of good memories. After all, Shiraz was the place I used to feel happy the most. My mother was delighted to see me. When she said, it was nice of me to come back so that she could see me again before she died made me feel quite disturbed. I told her she wasn't going anywhere and that she would live for another 100 years, at least.

After staying for a month in Iran, I couldn't avoid letting the bad and unsettling memories invade my mind. For how long could I've not possibly thought of what happened with me in Iran while I was in Iran? I guess this was inevitable. I should have thought this through before coming to Iran. That was a possible side-effect, and it was getting intense with each passing day. I started to feel the guilt and remorse for forsaking my kids. The shameful feeling was strong, and it took me by the storm within days. I felt like I had to get out of Iran, or else I would lose myself again.

Now that I think of the relapse, I feel it was a direct result of me just staying sober for five-and-a-half years and not getting proper treatment. At that time, I still had no idea I was suffering from chronic depression. I had attended support group meetings, but I had never been treated for depression.

I tried to calm myself down, but I couldn't. I could feel my anxiety, making me restless. Thus, I told my family I had to go back because of some business emergency. I made a promise to my sons that I would come back soon, and I left. I came back to Vancouver after almost a month and a half and started attending group meetings. I was afraid I might lose my sobriety and become reckless and discontent again because I was beginning to feel uncomfortable in my skin. I knew that feeling. I was familiar with it. When I felt that way, I was about to lose control over myself. And that's what happened.

One day, I was returning from a support group meeting, and I felt like smoking crack. In just one moment, my five and a half years of sobriety came to an end. I went back to drinking and smoking crack. As a result, I lost my business, bank balance, and my house within six months.

I guess unhealthy people attract unhealthy habits. Sick people attract sick people. That's what happened to me during this phase of mine. I met a working girl called Brandy. I was surprised to see how many details of our lives were similar.

Consequently, I developed a profound emotional connection with her. She taught me so much about humans, kindness, and suffering. When I was with her, I felt like I was a better person. The reason why we got along with each other was that she was also battling pain by using crack. Her life was miserable, just like mine. Her past haunted her, and she couldn't say no to her cravings, just like me. We became best friends and smoking and drinking companions. In fact, after losing my house, I moved in with her for some time.

There were incidents in Brandy's life that were far more distressing than mine. She was suffering from pain, misery, trauma, and multiple sexual assaults. Brandy was in the same situation as I was, maybe even worse. She told me her story, and I cried for her. I could feel her pain because I had gone through similar experiences in my life. We were more than just two people living together. We were two people who could understand each other in a way no one else could. Brandy was the first person I shared my guilt and sorrow. I told her everything, and she could relate to every single mishap and trauma of my life.

During the time I spent with Brandy, I got a chance to meet a lot of working girls. They used to sell their bodies for money, but my experiences with them weren't always sexual. What drew me closer to them was their stories. Each girl had a story that would touch your heart. All of them were in pain and leading a miserable life like me. To my surprise, these working girls were the only people who could understand me. We had nothing but compassion and love for each other. We used to care for each other. I developed a whole new level of respect for women in general, after meeting them. After listening to their traumatic stories and experiences with heroin and crack, I realized how devastating addiction could be.

Meeting these working girls and talking to them made me wish I was in a better state and could help each one of them. These women were someone's mothers, someone's sisters, and someone's daughters. They were human beings for me first. They were mothers, daughters, and sisters in my eyes, and then they were prostitutes. I didn't care if they were involved in a profession that is commonly frowned upon. They were real people. They were struggling. They were striving. And they were victims of the harshest and cruelest circumstances.

Some of these girls had families they hadn't seen in years. Some of them had kids they had left behind. They needed help and support, which nobody was willing to give them. In the months that followed, whenever I had money, I would give some of it to these girls, so that they didn't have to get picked up by any other guy for sex. If not money, I'd give them drugs, so they may calm their nerves and forget their worries for a while. I used to drive around in my car and help them out. They were in awe as to why I was helping them because nobody cared about them.

No one gives anything to anyone without expecting anything in return. That's the general principle that we live by in our lives. However, I was a nice guy. Even though I was suffering from severe depression and addiction, I wanted to help these girls because I connected with them on an emotional level.

For a very long time, I continued living with Brandy. One day, I decided it was more than enough, and I needed to get help. I told Brandy that I wanted my life back. And just like that, I joined the third detox center and stayed there for a few days.

Here's what my life had come to: I stayed sober for six months, nine months, or a year; I promised myself and my friends this time it's going to be different, but then I snapped in a moment. I knew the consequences of addiction. How it affected my business, my personal life, and relationships, but even then, I used to give in to my addiction. For six months, I would waste myself to the point I had nothing left to eat and no place to live, and I would go back to McDonald's to ask for food. Six months before that, I was living in a proper house with hundreds and thousands of dollars in my bank account. And then I would let everything slip through my hands. After attending the detox center, I denied any possibility of destroying my life with crack again. But just 15 minutes later, I would find myself buying crack at some shady corner of the street.

Addiction is a disease. It develops when you lose connection with the world around you. I got disconnected from reality and other human beings. My life lacked a more profound connection because of the chaos I had been through in my life.

I was going through one of the better phases of my life when Maryam, my younger sister, had me completely sold on the idea of getting married again. At that time, I was three months sober and was running my business. The girl she was trying to get me married to was from Iran, but I wasn't going there to meet her. Instead, we arranged for the meeting in Istanbul, Turkey. I rented a hotel room in Istanbul, and we lived there for a week, trying to get to know each other. For me, meeting a new person was difficult because I couldn't talk about myself. My childhood was not very pleasant. My youth was tainted with torturous events. And the story of my adult life didn't go beyond addiction to alcohol and crack. If truth be told, I did not know anything about love. I just thought marrying a nice woman would be a great idea to overcome my loneliness, which had become inconvenient. The girl I met was polite and caring, but the whole time I was with her, I felt I was not honest with her. I was keen on hiding my reality from her. I couldn't tell her about my problems and addictions that I had been battling with for years.

When I think about this marriage now, I feel it was a mistake. I acted upon Maryam's insistence and my desire to have a life partner. But was I mentally sound enough to marry a woman who didn't know anything about me? Was I fair with her? I think what I did was insane. Even the sanest person cannot marry someone after spending a week together.

In 2009, I went to Iran for two weeks to get married. It was a simple wedding, attended only by the close members of mine and my wife's families. A few days after I got married, I came back to Vancouver, while my wife stayed back in Iran. Her documents were not ready, and I had to take care of her paperwork that would take six months. When I arrived in Vancouver, I realized the business I had left with a friend of mine was not doing well and was on the verge of collapsing. As a result, I started drinking and using drugs again. I stayed under such a heavy influence of crack and booze that I disappeared from the face of the earth for one month. I didn't even call my wife in Iran and left her crying.

This behavior of mine disturbed me a lot. Deep down, I knew this girl I married didn't deserve what I was doing with her. I had promised her and her family that I will take care of her. But instead, I was going through one of my episodes. I started to feel ashamed and guilty, which forced me to stay drunk and doped even more. After wasting myself for about a month, I ended up in another treatment center. I started feeling better, but I still had no understanding of my addiction, trauma, and alcoholism. I didn't know why I went back to drinking and using crack. I didn't know why all the shame and guilt kept coming back intermittently. I knew I needed help, but I didn't know what exactly would help me if everything that I was doing hadn't helped me so far. The effect of all the support group meetings that I attended and detox centers that I went to lasted only for a few months. One day, I mustered my strength and called my wife in Iran. I didn't dare to confess my years' old addiction to crack and alcohol, so I told her a half-baked story in which I told her I had been facing some problems with alcohol lately. I told her I had already started the treatment, and that I'll be good in no time. She didn't know anything about me. She said her family was upset as to why I was not bringing her to Canada. However, she said she would wait for me to get better. What else could she have said? I came out of the treatment center and had a relapse after a few days. After that, I went to five or six detox centers.

My friend of the last 15 years, Savey, helped me a lot at every step of the way. His dedication and willingness to see me healed and healthy gave me the strength to continue battling my addictions. He was an excellent source of inspiration for me. But above all else, he was an amazing and caring human being. After I left the treatment center, Savey even helped me build my business again.

It took my wife two and a half years to get to Vancouver. By then, I was sober for nine months and had a business that was running smoothly. I had a good bank balance, and I was happy that my wife was finally coming to live with me. She hated me because of what I had put her through for the last two-and-a-half years. However, I knew I was going to be gentle and affectionate to her and prove myself to be the husband she thought I would be. My wife came to Canada in 2011. I picked her up from the airport in my new Ford SUV and brought her home. It turned out that my wife had huge expectations of me. She thought Canada would be like a paradise and that I would be living in a mansion. In reality, I was living in a 500 or 600 square feet apartment. To make sure she kept herself busy and had something to do, I offered her to start working at my office. She approved of the idea and started working.

Back then, I was eleven months sober and had $200,000 in the bank. Then one night after my wife had been here for three months, I felt the urge to smoke crack again. I couldn't resist the temptation, and nobody in the world could stop me. I lied to my wife that I was going to Seattle to take care of a business matter and ended up in a downtown Vancouver hotel to smoke crack and drink. I kept lying to her for two weeks that I will come tomorrow, but that tomorrow never came.

I told her it would take another day for me to return, but I never went back. My wife was worried sick about me and left hundreds of messages, asking where I was and what was I up to. She left messages that I had to come back as soon as possible because the business was going down, but I couldn't care less. There were people, office staff, and technicians who worked for me and were depending on me, but I didn't care.

I returned home after two weeks to an angry wife and a business that had crashed as a result of my relapse. My employees had left. However, I still had some money in my bank account. I started by saying sorry, but that didn't work. I lied to her and denied everything about what she accused me of doing, but that also didn't work. Thus, I rented a 2-bedroom 2000 or 3000 square feet penthouse for us to make it up to her. After that, I took her to Cuba for a week. It was a vacation well-spent. We enjoyed spending some time together. However, that didn't stop me from drinking and using crack. My wife sensed something was severely wrong with me. She spent hours crying and continued living a sad life, seeing me come home either drunk or high. After a few months, she could not put up with me anymore and said, *"I want a divorce."*

Khula is what Muslims call a divorce when a woman initiates the divorce proceedings. After all that I had made her suffer, this was the least I could give her. I put some money in her bank account, enough for her to rent a basement suite, and arranged for her to work with my friend's wife at a local pizzeria because she didn't want to leave Canada. It hurts my heart and makes me sad to this day when I think of what I put her through. Years later, I got to know that she remarried and now has a daughter.

I was happy for my wife that she was moving forward in life. As for me, I was walking the same road to destruction that I often walked in troubled times. I was not new to walking this road. After my wife left, I went crazy. The bolt of loneliness struck me again, and I couldn't take it anymore. My addictions got worse, I lost all my money, and I became homeless in just four months.

This time, my addictions went way out of control. They used to be bad, but never this bad. This time, I thought I would never recover. It was as if a strange darkness was taking over me, and I was losing track of everything around me. For the first time so far, I felt scared of myself, of what

I had become. This time I wasn't able to give up my addictions until five years ago when I was in this despicable hotel, called "Cobalt."

My room was infested with cockroaches and mouse, but I didn't care as long as I had crack to smoke and booze to drink to drown my sorrows. I was in the same filthy hotel when I received a call from my sister, Aktar. She was informing me that my elder son was getting married in a few days. My whole family wanted me to attend the wedding at any cost. Akhtar said, *"You weren't there in his life, every time your son needed a father; so you have to come now. It will make him happy."*

I said I would come. After all, it was my son's wedding, and this was my chance to prove my love for him. The only problem was that I didn't have any money. I asked my sister for some money, and she sent me $3,000. I collected the money and bought a ticket for myself. I was delighted that I was going to attend my son's wedding and will be able to make it to his special day. Just three hours before I was to leave the hotel, I felt like I couldn't get up. I picked up another drink and smoked another crack, but that made me feel worse. How was I supposed to control my addictions over there in front of everyone? Was I even fit enough to attend my son's wedding? I'm such a disgrace, what if I end up ruining my son's wedding with my presence? All these stupid questions flooded my mind, and I kept smoking crack and drinking booze. One glass after another, one crack joint after another, it was as if I wouldn't be able to stop. I might die of an overdose.

I ended up missing my son's wedding. An hour and a half later, I went and canceled the ticket. I got a refund because I wanted money to drink more. The fact that my mother, sister, and two sons were waiting for me in Tehran kept bothering me. They had traveled from Esfahan to pick me up from the airport, and I was drinking myself to death in a shitty hotel room that stank. I didn't have the guts to call them and tell them I won't come to Iran out of shame and guilt. I cried and cried and listened to sad Iranian music all night long. I felt lost thinking, why was this happening to me? I noticed there was a mouse in the room, not very far from where I was sitting, and it kept watching me. I started talking to the mouse and shared my feelings with it. My life became so small that at that time, the mouse became my best friend.

Whenever I drank and smoked crack, I preferred my room to be dark. So I got up on the chair to cover the light on the ceiling with my shirt, trying to make the room darker. I couldn't reach the light, so I left my shirt on a fire sprinkler. I thought I would never be able to get out of this hotel.

Luckily, one of my friends, Benny, called me, and when I didn't answer his five or six calls, he came to the hotel to see if I was still alive. He knew where I was because I was living in this cheap hotel for quite some time now. When Benny arrived and saw my shirt on the ceiling, the first thing that came to his mind was that I was trying to hang myself. Benny informed my other friends about me, and soon Tony Roberts called and said, *"Essi, if you kill yourself, I won't come to your funeral."*

I was depressed and wanted to die out of self-pity. I never tried to hang myself or cut my wrists, but what I was doing with myself all these years was a suicide attempt. The desire to die, to end my life, never left me. At that moment, I felt I didn't deserve to lead a good life. I wasn't good enough for life to be good with me. I was so depressed and disconnected from the world around me that I could relate with people who blew themselves in suicide bombings. That was the same feeling that compelled me to volunteer in the war and become a child soldier. I had my whole life ahead of me back then, and I chose to blow myself into pieces. I had no will to live when I decided to become a child soldier, and I had no will to live when my friend came to get me that night. I figured the low self-esteem of mine was responsible for the failure of my relationships. Whenever I was in a relationship,

I couldn't stop thinking that I was not good enough for the girl I was with. I used to guess what was she doing with me? I was not good for her. What could I possibly give this girl I was dating? I had nothing to offer her.

Lying in that hotel room in a miserable condition, I felt ashamed of myself in front of my friend. I was tired of feeling ashamed and guilty. Throughout my adult life, I felt my addiction had chained my feet, and I was unable to move ahead. Thus, I made a little prayer at that moment. I asked Jesus, Buddha, Allah, or whatever higher entity that was watching over me to help me. *"I can't do this anymore,"* I said in my prayer. *"I can't live like this any longer. And if that's how the rest of my life would be, I don't want to live anymore. Just give me death."*

That night Jason and Lisa took me to their house. They gave me some food to eat, and I took a shower and then I went to bed. The next day, I went to the treatment center. And this time, I gave it all I had. I followed every instruction, and I saw a psychiatrist as well. I had seen psychiatrists before, but I never really had any hope. But this time, the impact of me hurting my family and missing my son's wedding was too strong. I was sick and tired of being sick and tired until I was introduced to the 12-step program, which changed my life. This program helped me realize I don't want to be a victim anymore. That brought the turning point in my life. Until that night at Cobalt, my addiction wasn't hurting anyone, like my mother, sister, or sons. It was hurting only me. But this time, I hurt my family, and I felt shattered after doing what I did. I never wanted to feel like that again. As much this incident was humiliating and devastating, it was a turning point in my life. This time I wanted to change. I decided to give my 100% and change my life. So, I also started going to a trauma group, and I started seeing an alcohol addiction counselor every week and sometimes a couple of times a week.

I first went to another treatment center where I spent two months; that's where I started following the 12-step program. Besides the program, I started going to the gym, started working, and quit smoking. I also started helping other people in the treatment center. Everybody in the program knew me because of all the pain, suffering, and treatments that I had gone through.

The 12-step program was indeed a game-changer for me. The best thing that the program did was it made me admit that I have a problem to deal with. For someone who had spent 20 years being an addict, it's a slightly tricky thing to accept because we enter this lifestyle with pride and ego. I had the intention to get sober and healthy all the time. Still,

I couldn't work toward achieving that goal until I joined the 12-step program, which helped me stop feeling victimized. The program made me stop thinking that everybody did this to me. Poor me, I had to go through so much at such a young age.

You see, these sympathetic feelings for yourself don't help you at all. These feelings make you feel sorry for yourself. And self-pity is your biggest enemy. The first step I had to take was to identify and admit I have a problem. And for that, I had to let go of self-pity. I reached out to all the positive influences in my life to win some sense of accomplishment and stop feeling sorry for myself. I contacted Savey and some other friends I had made. One of them was a guy called Tony, who was sober for many years. Juggy, a good friend of mine, was another. However, Savey was the one who took an interest in me the most and did whatever he could do to help me and see me stand on my feet again. He often went out of his way to help me. He took me to his home a couple of times, and let me spend some quality time with his wife and his family. He started making me feel I was a part of his family.

Once you have given up on pitying yourself and have realized that you have a problem to deal with, you get to move on to step 2, which suggests that there is a solution to that problem. Thus, to find a solution, I started following the 12-step program and attending trauma support meetings. In these meetings, I came across people struggling with the same problem as mine. Some of them had recovered and were leading a decent and productive life. Back in those days, I was listening to a lot of inspirational people, like Tony Robins. I was following people like Oprah Winfrey. Oprah became my idol. I was highly motivated when I heard her talk about *I am responsible for my actions*. She made me believe that everything I need to do is for me. I cannot expect the same from anyone. I listened to those videos and realized that it was my time now. I had to stop blaming it on the government or anybody else. That, for me, was the solution to my problem.

It was time for me to follow step 3, which was about making a decision. For me, making a decision was all about willing to work on myself through the rest of the steps toward personal betterment. Step 4 required me to write down the names of all those people who I resented, hated and felt anger for. My list included a lot of names: my father because he separated me from my mother; my stepbrother, who bullied me around when we were kids; my brother-in-law, who used to beat me like an animal; the guy who assaulted me in the truck; all those racist Germans who taunted and teased me for being an impoverished Iranian refugee; and the Iranian government for ruining my childhood by brainwashing and forcing me to fight in the war. That was the easy part - to figure out how each person on the list affected me, my self-esteem, and my ability to interact with other people. The challenging part was to make healthy relationships. When I figured all that out, I realized no wonder I wanted to kill myself. I started taking counseling and sharing my feelings and guilt with professionals. It was a tough thing to do, but it had to be done. I had to let the past get out of my system. Thus, I started sharing my experiences with people I trusted and knew won't judge me, like Savey and Tony, who were my sponsors at the treatment center. I started praying, but not to the god I was taught to pray in my childhood. I started praying to a higher power, a loving God. I also started exercising regularly.

In steps 5 to 9, I had to share with my sponsor experiences of mine that induced self-pity and were blocking me from being happy. I had to share all those events that made me blame others, made me resentful toward others, and made me feel guilty and ashamed. I had to find someone and share everything with that person. I had to be honest with him. I did that, and it was a huge step forward and a turning point in my life. I started developing some self-esteem. I started believing I was not a victim. Yes, all those terrible and appalling things happened to me, but now, it is my responsibility to take care of myself. Thus, I started making amends with people I was unfair with, like both my wives and sons. I apologized and made things right with people. That strengthened my self-esteem. I stepped out of my comfort zone and started sharing my story with different people, and they asked me to go and speak at different places. When I did that, I had people coming to me saying, *"Hey Essi, you inspire me. You make me believe my life is not as bad as I thought it was."* You won't believe it, but people asked me to be their mentor. I walked them through what I went through. As a result, I started developing a sense of being useful. I went to the gym and worked out every day. I prayed; I meditated; I never missed my appointments with my psychiatrist. And that's how I treated my depression.

With that, I qualified to enter the last phase of the 12-step program. In steps 10, 11, and 12, I was taught that my whole life is built on relationships with other people; including friends, romantic partners, coworkers, and parents, etc. And it's highly likely that someone, including myself, would ruin these relationships because people have defects. They are not perfect. People hurt us, crush us, and disappoint us all the time. But the key is how I deal with all these setbacks in life.

I was told not to let the effect of these setbacks build up inside me till they explode, and that I need to make amends when I make a mistake or when I get upset. I learned that doing so doesn't make me a weak person. It makes me a stronger and more courageous person because it takes courage to admit mistakes. That's why I thank people or say sorry to them when I must. I now always straighten things out with people before they get worse. Our mind is like a bottle. If we continue keeping resentment and anger in it, it will blow up. And that's precisely what happened with me time after time after time, and that's why I ended up going to 17 treatment centers and 29 detox centers. The reason why my illness got prolonged is that I never really did house cleaning. Our mind is like a fridge filled with vegetables and fruits, and if we don't take care of these vegetables and fruits, they will eventually rot. If we go and top the fridge up with new grocery to make the refrigerator look clean and well-maintained from the outside, the rotten vegetables and fruits that are buried inside would affect the whole grocery, and the fridge will smell once again. It's an analogy that explains you have to timely resolve all your previous issues and problems that cause anger and resentment, instead of letting them pile up inside you.

The efforts I put into the 12 step program earned me a nomination for the "Courage to Come Back Award." Vancouver Coastal Health presented me with that award to celebrate my sobriety.

Today, I talk about the incidents of my life openly in public - how I shot myself in the war, how I got molested in the back of the truck, and how I endured a brutal domestic beating. Whenever I talk about these incidents, similar stories always come up, which makes me realize I wasn't the only one who got affected by these incidents. There are so many people like me who have gone through the worst phases of their lives, without sharing the tragedies of their life with anyone. I help them speak up. And that makes me feel I can bring a constructive change in their lives. That's the purpose of life I was seeking all my life. I talk on radio shows, I give interviews, I give motivational speeches, and I listen to the good, bad, and ugly stories of people from around the world on different platforms. I allow people to share their experiences, feelings, fears, insecurities, achievements and struggles to help them out. Just so they don't fall for the same addictions, I fell for in response to my horrible experiences. I've mentored and helped lots of people in the last 20 years, which is nothing short of an achievement. I try to inspire people with my words on radio stations in British Colombia, New York, and Pittsburgh. I have also given an interview on AM970 New York, a radio station that attracts a vast audience.

I learned that I could not forget all the pain that I went through in life, but that doesn't mean I should waste my life. I have a choice to change my life. I believe that I, as a human, was put on this earth by God for a reason. I got into so many fatal incidents that I shouldn't be alive, but I am alive for a reason. That reason is to share my pain and experience with others and help them out. People ask me to speak and inspire them in different cities and schools by sharing my experiences. People come to me and say, "Wow, my life is troubled and difficult, but after listening to you, you made my day." I share with them how they can be kind to each other and themselves. I tell them to believe that the glass is half full, but not empty. I ask them to focus on things they have to be grateful for.

The biggest lesson I learned from my experiences was that even if I make mistakes, which I make every day, I have the power to make amends because I don't want to hurt people or put them in pain. I don't want to be a part of someone's misery. So am I doing a perfect job, every time? No. But am I willing to learn and be a better person every day? Yes. Do I think about myself, 24x7? No. Do I think of myself most of the time? Yes, because that's human nature. I'm trying to do the best I can, to be of service to others. I ask myself, how can I make this world a better place? I want to tell people not to give up. I've made that my mission.

I speak in schools to teenagers and talk to them about how they can overcome their fears and their torturous past. I'm trying to start this thing called "Preventing Radicalization and Stop People from Getting into Gangs." I want to visit more and more schools in the U.S. and Canada, and talk to students and help the ones who are dealing with troubled past. I want to raise awareness that one should not give in to their fears and hardships. I believe families have a significant role to play. So, families should help troubled kids and involve them in social activities that keep them away from joining gangs or orchestrating mass shootings at schools or suicide bombings. I'm mentoring ten people personally. I'm helping them overcome their obstacles in life, like addiction, trauma, and self-esteem issues. We can get through addiction and sickness.

If we get beaten to the ground, we can always get up. We can still rise from our ashes, like a phoenix. That's my motto based on my personal life.

I want people to learn from my personal experiences and not make the same mistakes I made. My story does not belong to me. It's an example for others. It's an example that proves we need each other in troubled times. Human connections are a huge part of what I am today. Why do you think people pay for seminars and groups? They pay because they feel connected with other people. It makes them feel better.

There's a saying that goes like, "No matter how far down the scale we have gone, we will see how our experience can benefit others." I see the accurate reflection of this saying when I speak in different organizations, and people come to me and tell me how I have helped them change their lives. My reward is the fan mail I get, the messages I receive on social media, and the light I see in people's eyes after I touch them with my words. All of this gives me the courage to be more willing and do more for people than my financial situation allows me to do.

I want to emphasize that I do certain things every day. And this is what I do. I get up, and I pray and do what's in front of me. It's better to set a goal and live in the present and think about the future than to live in the past and keep on sulking and thinking "poor me, why these things happen to me?" As long as you feel like a victim, you cannot grow. You cannot lead a happier and healthier life. I get up, make my bed, and write a gratitude list of what I'm thankful for. Today, I have a lot of things to be grateful for. My health and sobriety always top the list. Now, I focus on how I can help other people. It's a significant change because my whole life I was inconsiderate and thought of myself only. However, that's not the case today. I have people that count on me. They want to share their struggles with me and ask me how I overcame my addiction. I don't tell them what to do. I share my experiences with them. I tell them how I overcame the epic obstacles in my life.

I have lived more than 50 years of my life, and I need more to be a better and kinder person. When I see humans do questionable things, I don't see them the way I used to. I don't judge them, and I analyze them as if something might be going on in their lives because that was the case with me. I did questionable things because there was something horrible going on in my life. My life experiences severely wounded me. It's safe to say that my experiences have changed my perspective entirely.

Before starting on my recovery journey, I couldn't control my emotional nature. I had trouble with relationships, I couldn't make a living, I had a feeling of uselessness, I was unhappy, and I was full of fear. Today, I'm different. I'm useful to other people, and I'm happy. I have a mission. I have the power of imagination. I mean, this is the same guy who hated himself and his life and wanted to die.

I have discussed most of my life with my sons. They understand me better than I thought they would when they would grow up. My sons have grown up to become intelligent and successful. For that, I owe my gratitude to Mehry's father. My older son is now married and runs a pharmaceutical business. Their grandfather raised them quite well and made sure that they turn into responsible young men. I love both my children. And at that time, I was filled with guilt and shame about what I had done. I could not reconcile my love for them with the actions that I had taken. I was just a man torn into two.

There's something I'd like to tell you about myself. It's personal, but I think it's essential if I share it with you. I'm not a political guy, so I can't say I don't like Iran. I love the country I belong to. I love Iran. The treatment I went through made me think about my country again. I don't want to blame the Iranian government either for what it did to me. I love Iranian people and how hospitable we are. I still have a family in Iran. They are Muslims, and there's nothing wrong with it. There's nothing wrong with Islam either. There's extremism in every religion, and I don't like that. I am open to experiences. I go to church, and I go to a Buddha's temple because I'm trying to find a religion that I can practice more. That's what step 11 of the program taught me, to improve my conscious contact with God. Thus, to do that, I'm trying to learn new things, and I have started going to church a lot. I'm trying to learn more about Christianity. Maybe Islam doesn't resonate with me because I could never speak Arabic.

Just like me, this book is also not political. It's a memoir. It's about my experiences and my opinions. Above all, this book is about hope. The light you see at the end of the tunnel is not a train. It is about presenting a possibility for people who need uplifting. I learned a lot from my experiences. Life is not easy. It's challenging, like a river, and we're like a boat that gets stuck, but then moves forward with a gentle blow of the wind or the push of a wave.

I couldn't be a productive member of society all my life, but now that I am in a condition to change people's lives, doing what I do is an honor for me. I feel honored when people and organizations invite me to their events. It's a rare gift. I don't deserve to be respected and recognized. It's a gift that has been given to me that I have to pass on. I'm grateful *for that. Thus, I won't stop doing what I do. I believe this is just the beginning of my journey.*

I've come a long way in my life. I've seen things. I've been around, and I've suffered.

I'm a survivor!